WILD TO THE HEART

WILD TO
THE HEART

Rick Bass

Drawings by Elizabeth Hughes

STACKPOLE BOOKS

Published by
STACKPOLE BOOKS
Cameron and Kelker Streets
P.O. Box 1831
Harrisburg, PA 17105

Printed in the United States of America

10 9 8 7 6 5 4 3 2 1

Excerpts from "A Tree, A Rock, A Cloud" from *The Ballad of the Sad Cafe and Collected
Short Stories,* by Carson McCullers. Copyright 1936, 1941, 1942, 1943, 1950, 1951,
1955, by Carson McCullers. Copyright © 1979 by Floria V. Lasky, reprinted by
permission of Houghton Mifflin Company.

Reprinted from *Robert Frost and Sidney Cox: Forty Years of Friendship* by William R.
Evans, editor, by permission of University Press of New England. © 1981 by Trustees
of Darmouth College.

Library of Congress Cataloging-in-Publication Data

Bass, Rick, 1958–
    Wild to the heart/Rick Bass.
        p.   cm.
    Contents: Shortest route to the mountains–Paying dues–On
camp robbers, rock swifts, and other things wild to the heart–
Good day at Black Creek–Sipsey in the rain–Burrisizing–
Magic at Ruth Lake–Grizzly cowboys–Birthday party–Fish fry–
River people–First snow–Strawberries.
    ISBN 0-8117-1876-X
    1. Nature.   2. Outdoor life.   I. Title.
QH81.B319   1987
508-dc19   87-19394
                                                                 CIP

For my parents, and with thanks to Nancy Williams, Tom Lyon, and Moyle Q. Rice.

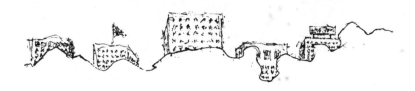

I lead a life estranged from myself. . . . I am very wild at heart sometimes. Not confused. Just wild–wild. . . .

Robert Frost

Contents

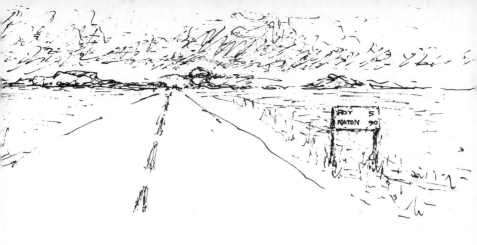

1

Shortest Route to the Mountains

THE TROUBLE WITH buying a strawberry milkshake from the Lake Providence, Louisiana, Sonic Drive-In on the left side of Highway 65 going north through the Delta, north to Hot Springs, Arkansas, is that you have got to tag the bottom with your straw and then come up a good inch or so if you want to get anything, the reason being that the Lake Providence Sonic uses real strawberries and lots of them in their shakes. You stick your straw down to the bottom the way you do with other shakes and you won't get anything – your straw gets mired and plugged up in an inch or so of fresh-cut strawberries. So to get the actual shake itself moving up the straw and into your mouth you've got to raise the straw an inch off bottom, sometimes more, depending on who made the shake. If you've got a lot of time to kill, the best thing to do is to pull into the parking lot under the shade of

the big live oak that sprawls over and cools all of the Lake Providence
First Baptist Church and most of Highway 65 as well. (Years ago, the
phone company had planned to nip some of the larger limbs back
away from the highway because a storm might knock them down
onto the phone wire, but a petition was quickly circulated and signed
that requested the phone company not cut the limbs; the towns-
people would, said the petition, rather do without phone service for
a day or two than have the big tree's limbs pruned. There were 1,217
signatures on the petition; Lake Providence and the surrounding
hamlets of Oak Grove, Louise, and Rolling Fork have a combined
population of 1,198. The limbs were spared).

Parked under the big oak, you can still keep an eye out on the Sonic
because it is right across the street. The reason you want to keep an
eye on the Sonic is so you will know when the lady who puts more
strawberries in the shakes than the other ladies comes on duty. The
tag on her red-and-white uniform says "Hi, my name is Ellen." You
will know it is her when she drives up because she drives an old white
Dodge Dart with license plates that say "Ellen."

The best thing to do once you have ordered, paid for, and received
your milkshake, is to walk back over to the big oak and enjoy it over
there—early August is the best month to do this. But if you are in a
hurry to be off, if you are in a hurry to get to the mountains, you roll
your window up after paying Ellen (you stay in your car and order
through a loudspeaker—she brings it out to you and then waves
good-bye and says "Come back again" when you drive off) and you
move on, drinking the shake as you roll once more through the
Delta, ducking involuntarily every now and then as a crop duster
swoops head level across the highway. It is not the fastest route to the
mountains, nowhere near it—the quickest and most efficient path is
to jump up on the interstate and set the cruise control and rocket
out of Jackson through MonroeRustonShreveportTylerDallas-
FortWorthWichitaFallsAbileneAmarilloRatonPassDenver. But this
year I was not in a hurry to get to the mountains, because I had saved
up all of my vacation and was going to squander it all on this one trip;
two week's worth of freedom back in the state of my rebirth, two
weeks of freedom in the state that I love most but that is, unfortu-
nately, the least realistic state for me to make a living in. So I took the
route up through the Delta. It is not the fastest route to the mountains, but it is the shortest, the best.

Even after Lake Providence is long ago a speck in the rearview mirror, the pleasant strawberry taste of the milkshake lingers, and my stomach continues to make contented little strawberry-tasting rumbles. It is sinfully pleasurable to drive through this part of the country in August with the windows up and the air conditioner on and one of Ellen's milkshakes empty in the little bag in the front seat. Because in August the north Louisiana/Mississippi/south Arkansas Delta is the most unbearable spot on the face of the earth. The humidity remains at one hundred percent twenty-four hours a day, and the temperatures never dip below 105 until after the sun goes down.

With the exception of the lean, gaunt, anchored-to-tractors farmers who grow soybeans and cotton out of the rich floodplain deposits, in August the human race disappears. Even the wildlife is missing in August; only the toughest, most ancient life forms remain. Dragonflies buzz in one place over a small irrigation ditch, sometimes just hovering, waiting for the summer to end. And like interlopers, domesticated outcasts who have no business being in this hellhole, stocky black Angus stand motionless in the few fields that do not grow soybeans; except for the ever-swishing tails, when viewed from a distance, the cattle look like thick stout china imitations placed out in the fields to break the monotony (the monotony of money–this is the richest farmland on the planet). Only the reptiles flourish, as they always have. Red-eared sliders scramble across the sun-baked asphalt, wishing (as much as is possible for turtles to wish) that they could stop and bask an hour or two on the warm road but knowing they can't, that if they do then after about thirty minutes a big truck coming up from Jackson or New Orleans carrying a load of fryers to Little Rock (white feathers trailing behind it, swirling and fluttering in its wake) will come pounding down the highway, screaming and rattling and roaring and double-clutching and shaking the heat-buckled narrow two-lane that is already as warped as a Burma bridge, hellbent for Eudora or McGehee or Star City or any other little town that is fortunate enough to get in their way. The turtles have learned (as much as it is possible for turtles to learn) that those of their numbers who stay and bask in the pleasant August torpor of Highway 65 are almost inevitably flattened. A few of the luckier ones are only struck on the side-rim of their flat low-slung mossy carapaces by the truck's hub, and these are the ones that, rather than being squashed, are instead sent skittering head-over-teacups off the road and back into the ditch with only superficial injuries, where, with luck, they live to snap at dragonflies another day.

There is a great deal of satisfaction to be experienced in racing past the half-turned fields of cotton and soybeans barefooted in shorts and a tee shirt at two-thirty in the afternoon on your vacation, on your way through the Delta, on your way to the mountains, being able to watch the rest of the world at work while you and only you flaunt your two week's exempt status like a hard-earned badge, like a reward. It is as if you have escaped from a prison in some clever, cunning manner; it is a good feeling.

There is also satisfaction to be had in driving past the fields and watching the tractors raising clouds of dust that, if you are lucky and are on the tail end of an early Indian summer front, drift slowly toward Jackson and New Orleans under an exhilarating mock-October royal blue sky, even in August. But more years than not, the year's first crispness doesn't come until Thanksgiving weekend, the weekend of the big games, and on August Friday afternoons like this one the dust clouds raised by the tractors blow hot and dry toward Little Rock and Memphis, or at best mushroom up around the tractor like thick fog before wisping straight up into nothing. Going north to the mountains through Lake Providence, Louisiana, is not the fastest route to the mountains, but it is the best. It gives you time to think and to prepare for their beauty. It makes them seem more beautiful when you finally do get there.

Reed, population 403. Junction City, 377. Tillar, 273. There is a state park a few miles west of Tillar, but if you have left Jackson at noon and stopped for the strawberry shake in Lake Providence, then by now it will be getting close to four o'clock in the afternoon—sullen purple clouds will be pouting overhead where before, earlier in the day, there were no clouds—and it will be only an hour or two away from the hottest part of the day in the Delta—so you drive on.

Arkansas City, Arkansas, where, if you are still speeding north on the same flattened-turtle-shell-littered, flat-but-warped two-lane Highway 65 around four-thirty in the afternoon, lost in a song on the radio and half asleep, half hypnotized by the hum of your wheels and by the fast flat stretch of narrow Delta road, likely as not you can suddenly look up and focus on the battered rear end of an old farm truck's tailgate that is looking back at you and getting bigger fast. The truck's turn indicator lights will have been broken out many years ago, many many years ago, during the loading of an unruly Brahman bull calf into the back to take to auction, else they would be signaling a left turn. Your shoulders will widen and tense, your whitened knuckles gripping the steering wheel like a tourniquet, and on this particular stretch of 65 a few miles north of Mitchelville (494), almost in the Arkansas City city limits, if the driver of the old farm truck notices that you are bearing down on him, he will, likely as not, stop in the middle of his abbreviated left turn and gape into his rearview mirror, fascinated, as if not realizing it is he and not some stranger that is about to be rear-ended. The reason he is fascinated is that by and large, with few exceptions, an accident is a big event in Arkansas City, even if the person watching the accident is involved in it himself. Anything is welcome as long as it breaks the horrible monotony that sets in around August as they near the end of a long hard planting-and-harvesting season, a monotony spawned by almost six months of working dawn till dark in weather that never goes below one hundred degrees. So that others may eat. A car wreck, even your own, is much better than another day of work, come August and the end-of-summer fatigue.

But on this particular stretch of Highway 65 you come out of your hypnosis just in time; you whip the steering wheel around and pass on the right, on the shoulder, with inches to spare, and loose gravel scrambles out from under the tires and clatters up against the sides of your car, and then you are back up on the road again and the stopped truck is in your rearview mirror, its driver watching open-mouthed as you race north toward the mountains, no longer sleepy . . .

The scenery is hot. It is flat and drab, and you look at your road map for the fifth time in thirty minutes to see if you can look ahead and tell where it will end. You yawn and sing along with the radio even if you have never before heard the song that is playing; you do isometric exercises against the steering wheel; you roll the window down and then roll it back up again just to be moving. You read the billboards when you are lucky enough to pass one.

Sammie's Bait and Groceries – Mealworms, Earthworms, Cold Beer and Crickets. Stuttgart, Arkansas – Duck Hunting Capital of the World. Dumas, Arkansas – Home of '75–'76 State 2A Champs. All along the road on either side there stand large metal buildings that sell and service tractors old and new. There are tractor stores on Highway 65 the way there are casinos in Las Vegas. Massey-Ferguson, International Harvester, Stribling-Puckett. John Deere. Caterpillar. Cat. They are great strong red beasts (sometimes green) that, along with the men who run them, work from two hours before dawn until two hours after dusk six days a week for the rest of their lives with only an occasional oil change or a day off for maintenance.

North of Dumas the landscape is broken up a little by numerous small square muddy stock tanks. Catfish. Humphreys County, Mississippi – Catfish Capital of the World. Cotton is no longer king; cotton and cattle have been replaced by soybeans and catfish. Except for rabbits, I am told there is no other more efficient assimilator of protein than a channel catfish. University professors at agricultural schools throughout the South have estimated that by the year 2000, catfish will be the number one food crop in the United States, the number one food crop in the world. The land will be given a breather as crops are turned under for a few years so that stock tanks can be dozed up. Towns like Dumas will be rich. So say the scientists. In the meantime, Dumas waits. And grows catfish. Big catfish. But the catfish stay submerged, sulking down in the mud, getting fat on corn meal and cottonseed and rarely if ever show themselves; the scenery remains drab. You start yawning again.

Dooville, Arkansas, pop. 525. Where, upon filling the order for the three-piece dinner at the Dooville Chicken Basket, the woman at the counter puts not one and not two but five of the little double-barreled paper break-open vials of salt in the sack along with your order, since the news that salt causes high blood pressure has yet to reach Dooville. There are a lot of things that have yet to reach Dooville, a lot of things that probably never will, including high blood pressure itself.

Tamo. The Tamo water tower is somewhat unique from other water towers across the United States in that it has no graffiti on it, no Jerry-loves-Ginny, no Srs. of '76, no Tamo-Wildcats-Number-One. The reason for this is that there are no Tamo Wildcats. Tamo, Arkansas, has exactly seven (7) school-aged children, three of whom will graduate high school next year: two are going out to Texas to work on oil rigs, the third is going to the University of Arkansas on a basketball scholarship. The Tamo Seven attend school in Dooville, a fifteen-minute bus ride.

Other than the schoolchildren, the next-youngest people in Tamo are Gary and Shirley. They own Gary and Shirley's Grocery, one of six business establishments in the town of Tamo. Gary is thirty-three, Shirley thirty-four. Tamo, too, waits for the catfish boom.

Finally, at long last, the metropolis of Pine Bluff. Fifty-seven thousand plus. An Oasis of culture in the Arkansas wilderness. Mobile homes, the Silver Shocker Disco, Pat Kreeton Figure Salon, and the Giant Water Slide (Fastest in Arkansas!). Have a Coke and a Smile. A-1 Muffler Shop.

It would be easy to dislike Pine Bluff with its big-city sprawl of billboards and stop lights in the otherwise-relaxing south Arkansas farmland, but I notice that when I stop for gas at one of the local service stations – and this is more than I can say for the service stations in New York, Chicago, Los Angeles, and Cincinnati – the restroom is immaculate. Still, I hurry through Pine Bluff as fast as I can, getting lost and turned around in the wrong direction only twice. The last time I get lost pretty good, so that I finally end up not even knowing how to backtrack, and I stop and ask for directions outside a Kroger grocery store. Three old men with grey-stubble beards, retired farmers with all their daughters married off and their sons-left-home-too and nothing much to do are sitting out front as if waiting for someone to come by and ask them for directions.

A light rain has started falling, the kind that falls every day at this time in Pine Bluff in the summer – the fat pregnant purple heat-spawned thunderclouds build up all day long and then sprinkle down just enough each day to make the crops grow – and we stand there in the rain discussing my roots, because they ask me where I am from before I can get the question out. "From Jackson," I tell them. This makes no impression on them, and I realize that they are not familiar with Jackson. "From the South," I add. They mull this over; it seems to be inconceivable to them that I could have gotten lost. It occurs to me that this could very well be the first time anyone has ever gotten lost in their town and asked them for directions. They look at each other bemusedly, glad that it is I and not they who are lost, having no more idea than a hoot owl where 270 West is, or even if there is such a beast.

"I jes' get on the free-way and go," one of them chuckles to another, waving his arm in a wild carefree half circle that takes in a sweep of country somewhere roughly between Tacoma, Washington, and Minneapolis-St. Paul. I grimace, try to smile politely, thank them, climb back in my car, and take off in the general direction of the arc.

7:30 P.M. Skies are blue again, with only a few thin white wisps of clouds above. Already, however, they are building, and I know that by tomorrow evening they will once again be bunched together, fat and purple and bulging with rain, but this doesn't concern me; tomorrow I will be in the mountains, on vacation, where it never rains.

Dusk. Dragonflies from out of nowhere career off my windshield like soft-bodied bullets, speckling it green when they hit, colliding with such impact that, until you are conditioned to them, you wince at first and flinch each time one hits, as if it were something real and living you had just struck and not just an old dragonfly. But you get used to it.

Fairfield, Arkansas. No names on the Fairfield water tower, either.

Twilight, almost dark, and every small-town radio station in the South can be picked up now under the cover of darkness. You reach the outskirts of Hot Springs three hours later, where, bone weary and bleary eyed, you pull off the road to nap for a couple of hours before starting up again. You fall asleep dreaming summertime dreams of a girl you knew in high school a long time ago. This time tomorrow you will be in the mountains.

It is not the fastest route to the mountains, but it is the shortest.

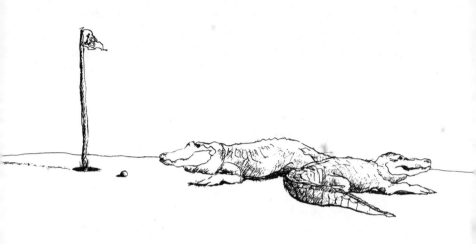

2

Paying Dues

LAST NIGHT I went to a Sierra Club banquet down on the coast. A friend of mine, a girl from work, had invited me. It was held in Ocean Springs, a tiny town set back across a drawbridge on the other side of a bayou in which wood ducks squeal and fly hard and fast through cypress forests and alligators groan and commercial fishermen catch salty-smelling gar and gasper-gou, but even though it was held in Ocean Springs, it was the mayor of Biloxi who muscled in and spoke rather than the O.S. mayor. Or perhaps Ocean Springs does not have a mayor; perhaps it is the Biloxi mayor they listen to, I don't know. The two towns are not far apart. I know that if I had my choice, I would rather live in Ocean Springs than in Biloxi, even if there isn't a mayor. Biloxi has an air force base and a shipyard and a mess of new shopping malls, plus lots of sea gulls and white sand and in the summertime lots of people. Ocean Springs has a lot of sea gulls too, and lots of pretty homes looking out onto the gulf, and in the summertime it gets more than its share of people too, but it also has the ducks and the alligators.

Once, or so the hostess of last night's banquet told me, a family of alligators moved up out of the bayou and lived on the Ocean Springs golf course and terrorized first-time golfers at the club by sunning lazily on the green of the eighteenth hole, eyes shut and jaws slack, basking as motionless as a row of pale serrated railroad ties, rousing only to skulk off and hide in one of the sun-warmed sand traps at the sound of an approaching golf cart. The hostess told me that after a particularly long drive, if a well-hit ball was to come bounding down the fairway the way it was supposed to do on the dogleg par five, rolling up onto the green and toward the pin, then sometimes (said the hostess) one of the little young alligators would dart out onto the green and snap it up as if it were nothing more than an extremely crunchy turtle egg. She said if you were close enough you could hear them crunching the golf balls, could hear the dog-clacking-on-a-bone noises they made as they gnawed on them with their grinning teeth, and right at dusk, you could sit up on the club's second-floor patio restaurant and look down on the eighteenth hole and see as many as five or six of them at a time: still, dark forms lying motionless on the lighter-colored fairway, waiting for morning.

Club members had even given them names–the hostess tried but could not remember what the names were; it had been several years– but not long after this, the alligators disappeared, as if disapproving of their new names, or perhaps unnerved at last by the old women of the club who would ride out during lunch in their own golf carts, entire convoys of them, riding out to throw poorly aimed day-old bread crumbs at the slumbering creatures, as if feeding goldfish in a pond or pigeons in a park, not knowing it was fish and duck eggs the gators longed for and not stale bread. I started to ask the hostess if she had been one of the crowd who had gone out daily to pelt the alligators with old croutons, but she anticipated my question and excused herself and moved hurriedly away, off to fill the punch bowl or perhaps tell the alligator story to someone else.

I asked someone else about it, another long-time Ocean Springs resident–he was not a golfer, I learned disappointedly–and he said that it was true, that they really had lived up on the golf course for a while, but that it had been several years ago, and that now the only alligators that live in Ocean Springs live back in the swamps, back down in the bayou itself—at night you can still hear them sometimes, in the summertime—but the wind has to be just right and you have to go pretty far back in the swamp to do it. Ocean Springs just kept getting bigger and bigger, he said sadly, and I could tell that he had not gone down in the swamp to hear the alligators in a long time.

I looked around the big room, looking for the girl I had driven down with, and found her by the fireplace, talking to one of the Club's—that was how they referred to it, as the Club, with a capital C—newsletter editors from up in the north part of the state. They were talking not about new record albums and not about counted cross-stitch, but rather, about sulfur dioxide emissions.

I moved in closer and caught snatches of the conversation. Not enough to figure out exactly what they were talking about, but enough to impress me that they had gone beneath the opening line superficialities of many first-time conversants (I learned later that until then they had never met, though at the time it would have surprised me: they were popping down peanuts and nodding yes, yes, and sipping white wine and laughing as if they had gone to school together, as if they were roommates) and instead actually knew what they were talking about.

". . . PSD Class I areas," I heard my date saying, and then a scrambled something from the other girl that was washed away by the roar of the party, followed by more distorted garble that ended with "senate majority" and "Office of Management and Budget." I moved on to the cheese dip.

The banquet, I suppose, went fairly well. The mayor of Biloxi was a good speaker, and inspiring. A member of the Club himself, he chose oddly enough not to applaud the efforts of a few but rather to criticize the non-efforts of many. We listened attentively. He spoke a little about one of his pet projects, a proposed intracity zoning ordinance that would require all new homes to have two separate and attractive compartments recessed into their kitchens somewhere: one for glass and one for aluminum. They would, he told us with great enthusiasm, quickly pay for themselves, and I thought that was a neat idea, much neater than the two ratty cardboard boxes I have stashed in the corner of my kitchen, much neater than strip-mining the American West for more ores when they could just as easily be recycled.

There are no alligators where I live, in Jackson, 150 miles to the north. Heart of the Sunbelt, Crossroads of the South, Jackson no longer has the time or the patience to put up with alligators on the links. There is a fine swamp of a river, the Pearl, that floods annually and bisects the very center of the town, snaking down out of the upland pine country and down through the Delta before emptying into the Big Water about twenty miles north of New Orleans – and it passes right under the main highway leading into Jackson, right under the main downtown street; you can see it from the top of almost any office building in town – but it has no wood ducks. The planes, the trucks, the cars, the excitement of urban growth – the wood ducks do not understand these things, so they avoid this section of the Pearl River.

Driving into town in the mornings, crossing the Pearl, I almost always see fishermen, retired people mostly, fishing back in the high-water coves and back bays in flat-bottomed john boats, and on weekends, in the summer, driving by at night, I see the glow from their lanterns sprinkled all up and down the river as they pole up and down the banks looking for the deep-bass-drumming bullfrogs that line the shores like small green boulders.

The swamp goes right up to the very fringes of the downtown district; it is as ideal a mix of the big city and the outdoors as one could ask for. Sometimes on my lunch hour, in the spring, I drive to work with my canoe on top, and ease out of the parking lot a few minutes past noon and put in at the State Street bridge and fish for a good forty minutes, all the while never losing sight of my tall spar-kling monolithic white-brick-with-gold-mirrors-for-windows office building; great red fiberglass letters perch atop the twenty-first floor, telling everyone that it is the Mississippi Bank building – they light up at night and glow in the dark to keep planes from crashing into them in the river-bottom fog – Hawkins Air Field is two miles to the north – and yet, despite this ideal mix, I grouse.

I grouse about the number of people moving into the town daily, I grouse about the potholes, I grouse about the EPA studies that showed shortly before the EPA's enforcement districts went extinct that Jackson's drinking water contained a concentration of trihalomethanes—tiny pollutants from upstream that combine with silt and other organic matter in the Pearl River to form carcinogens—that was two-thirds over what the EPA used to allow. I was born in Houston, Texas, Ur-Mother of all Big Cities, but went to school out West, up in the mountains, and got spoiled in the meantime.

I had a hard time adjusting to Jackson: for the first year or so, my dreams were haunted by red aspen leaves and the Blacksmith Fork of the Logan River. My letters to friends back up in the mountains were bitter and cynical, saying things like ". . . you'd like Jackson a lot, however. There are eight airports, one with jets—loud jets—and lots of rain and concrete and oh, Ken, you never saw so many red and green traffic lights. It's like Christmas all year round, it's really beautiful, you'd love it. And the scenery! Drugstore after drugstore after shopping mall after shopping mall . . ."

In time, however, I did adjust. I learned to change my thinking and appreciate things in Jackson the way I had in Utah. I put a bird feeder out by my apartment, and every morning now am awakened by the squabbles of bold and colorful blue jays. Instead of biking up the canyon to look for a moose between classes, I now take my coat off and change into tennis shoes and catch bream on a fly rod out of a muddy river basin in the heart of the downtown business district on my lunch break. Just last night I saw a beautiful luna moth on my door, a great pale velvety luminous-looking creature with long sweeping wings and huge feathered antennae; I was too afraid to try to shoo it away so I could go inside, too unsure of how to pick it up and move it—like a bachelor holding a crying baby, I would not have known how to do it, or where to put it—it looked too fragile—so instead I set my briefcase down and sat down and watched it for forty-five minutes, waiting for it to leave, before a big toad hopped up under the porch light and jumped up and snapped at it before I could do anything. The toad missed, jumped up again, and like a great crippled Boeing jet the moth wheeled clumsily around and flapped off into the woods, uninjured, and, seemingly, unfrightened.

And sometimes, driving to and from work, back in my neighborhood I see box turtles crossing the roads; not the same as seeing a coyote hurry across the highway, or a cow elk and calf, but, as I said, I have learned to adjust. I can handle it.

This is not to say that Jackson, Mississippi, is bad just because there are no coyotes or elk, just because alligators are not tolerated and the jackhammers scare away the wood ducks. On the contrary: Jackson, Mississippi, is good, very good, because it feeds me and keeps me and four hundred thousand other people alive and happy, which is more than my adopted wilderness area, the High Uintas of northern Utah, can say come blizzard time in December up above treeline. Jackson is a necessary good.

One of the things I noticed immediately at the banquet in Ocean Springs was how respectable everyone was. I don't mean yessir-nosir respectable, but the other kind: the banker-lawyer-clergyman kind. At first I had had reservations about coming to the banquet. "The Sierra Club," I said musingly when my friend first invited me. "Aren't they . . . aren't they . . . Don't they . . ." But I could not find the question I was looking for, so in the end I said yes, and bought not only my ticket but hers too. Perhaps at the banquet I would be able to figure out the question I was looking for.

Before the banquet, I had always sort of assumed in my mind's eye absurd and baroque stereotypes for any outdoor-oriented organization, never having been associated with one myself. Thus I came to picture members of the National Wild Turkey Federation not as the dedicated and extremely competent professionals they are, but instead as a group of good old boys dressed up in army boots and camouflage hunting suits, sitting in a posh convention room with their feet up on the tablecloth, leaning back in their chairs, practicing turkey calls across the room and swapping hunting stories while the waiters cringed and the maitre d's cowered as the turkey hunters laughed and joked and slapped their knees until it was time to go home, never once discussing the implementation of upcoming management activities. And the Sierra Club, I knew, had to be worse: long hair and sandals, goatees and granola bars, with the thick sour smell of marijuana hanging dusky-sweet everywhere, and furtive, whispered plans for anarchist plots and smokestack sit-ins in every conversation.

I was surprised. Men in suits and ties stood with arms crossed and talked not as I had imagined they would, not mumbling but instead talking coherently and intelligently of Senate Committees on Energy and Commerce and House Ways and Means Committees; beautiful women in long lavender evening dresses and pearl necklaces and honeysuckle perfume drifted from room to room, laughing and talking excitedly: they were as normal as any other congregation of people anywhere else in the world, and maybe more so. I was disappointed.

The banquet was being held at the Ocean Springs Country Club itself, the one that had had, for a while, gators in the family; before the talks began, even before the food was served, I walked out onto the darkened eighteenth hole—already the close-cropped grass of the putting green was damp and beaded with silver dew—and stood and waited and watched and listened—a hard breeze, a wind really, was blowing cold and wet from off in the gulf: I wondered if, downwind, they—the alligators, not the party goers—could smell me—and then, after a while, when the alligators did not appear, when they did not grunt and bellow for me, I went back inside, shivering, back out of the quiet and salty windy darkness and into the loud and bright and happy festivities of the clubhouse.

He went on to inform us that it was a good proposal and that a lot of people were in favor of it and furthermore it would never be passed. There was confused silence, and frowns—heads turned and looked around: did I miss something?—and then he explained. He explained that all too many organizations are writing letters and sending telegrams and donating money to their favorite outdoor causes, but that they are too selfish to donate their time. He said that this is what has led to the all-too-common stereotype of outdoorsmen being labeled "elitist": they send money and pay heavier taxes and buy special licenses and write their congressmen but when it comes time to pull up their sleeves and sit in cramped and stuffy high school auditoriums and testify, when it comes time to actually attend hearings and public meetings and go out and take their representatives by the arm and say look-here-this-is-what-I-want-how-can-I-get-it-what-can-I-do-what-committee-can-I-form, they go off pursuing their recreation, off hunting or hiking or fishing or camping.

Applause was absent-mindedly polite when he finished: it was not that it was a bad talk, it was just as if everyone were too sunk in his or her thoughts to clap really hard. It was as if they were thinking about the boring stuffy committees they knew they were going to have to volunteer to serve on now that they had been accused of not doing so. Now that they had been challenged.

The chapter chairman showed up late, dressed in a coat and tie but smelling of fish and swamp and outboard motor fuel—he and his wife had driven in from out of town and he had been out with a friend fishing all day while the wives toured the old homes. He said that their engine had cut out on them right at dusk, just as they were fixing to leave (just as the redfish were starting to run) but you could tell that it was an old story, you could tell that she, his wife, had heard it before. He gave a good talk, though, as good as the mayor's only more cheerful, and when he was through everyone clapped and then he pulled a name out of a box to see who would win the brand-new seventeen-foot fiberglass forest green Seda Scout canoe that was sitting patiently in the aisle, listing to one side on the plush country club carpet.

We (yes, my date had sold me one of those too, a one-dollar canoe-raffle ticket) had been eyeing it enviously all night and running our hands across its slick gunwales as we passed by it in the dessert line. The tickets were a dollar each, and the canoe had been sold to the Club at half cost by a local outfitting company: the money raised by the raffle—they had sold over fifteen hundred tickets—was going to various conservation projects throughout the state. Six hundred people strained eagerly forward, already in their mind's eyes gliding silently through a wooded forest in Maine, or bouncing crazily down a stretch of haystacking white water up in the mountains of North Carolina—everyone was sure he or she was going to be the winner, everyone from out of town had brought a canoe rack atop the car—but in the end all six hundred of them groaned, because a man from Ocean Springs who was not even present, who was not even a member of the Club, won.

There was a dance scheduled; a band began to warm up, striking a few smart and oddly discordant drum thumps—I frowned: my date had not told me there would be dancing—and after a brief, hurried discussion ("That's the main reason I came, to dance!" she wailed, looking down at her long black evening dress) I remembered that the car had been making a funny sound on the way down.

"I'm going to go check on it," I said.

"You do that," she said.

I went outside and sat down out on the green, my back propped up against the flag stick, and waited for the alligators. Above me, the little yellow "18" banner flapped and fluttered madly, buffeting back and forth against the pole, and I pulled my coat collar up and tried to stay warm. From the clubhouse, I could barely hear the band. I thought about the mayor's talk as I shivered.

In 1981, a group called Defenders of Wildlife fought for vital protection of the essential habitat of the threatened grizzly bear in the Cabinet Mountains area of Montana's Kootenai National Forest. This may or may not have been a good thing to do, depending on your stance concerning Montana grizzlies, but personally, I would have liked to have been in on the fight. Where was I and what was I doing when it was going on? Kayaking? Backpacking?

The Fred Bear Sports Club is currently promoting a letter-writing campaign to purchase from agricultural interests the last existing high-quality continuous tract of bottomland hardwoods in the United States, in the Tensas River region of northeast Louisiana. It was only by the merest of chances—I do not belong to the club, I don't even bowhunt—that I saw a stray newsletter down at the local library; I picked it up, read it, and on my lunch break the next day wrote not only the governor of Louisiana but the president of the United States and the secretary of the interior as well.

The World Wildlife Fund has supported 260 national parks and equivalent reserves on five continents.

The Wilderness Society, cofounded by Aldo Leopold, often works with and advises local and state governments on proposed hunting seasons based on biological management considerations and data gathered in the field.

The Audubon Society's chapters everywhere are noted for their plethora of field trips. My friend's local Sierra Club group is into canoeing, with some sort of outing scheduled at least once a month—sailing, kayaking, hiking, skiing, climbing, biking . . .

It seems to me, then, that the point is this: there is something for everyone. There is still much to be said for the pleasure of getting up at the crack of dawn and going out by yourself, or perhaps with only one other—a son, a daughter, a father—and photographing mule deer, waiting for them to come filing down a desert canyon in southern Utah.

I like to camp and hike alone, or with one or two other friends at most. But what about Thursday nights, and Saturday afternoons in May when the fish aren't biting but the mosquitoes are?

It is good to belong to a group, a group that reflects accurately your own beliefs, a group that you can give suggestions and advice and ideas to, a group that allows one to, pardon the cliche, get involved. My friend from the office did not learn about PSA Class I areas in her on-the-job training as a medical secretary; her friend by the fireplace did not learn about the Office of Management and Budget in her job as a high school volleyball coach. They belonged to an organization that informed them and allowed them to formulate a collective voice on the issues of their choosings. Guiltily, I ask myself what I have learned. That the life span of a grizzly is four to twenty years? That the best way to catch brook trout in the spring in the Blacksmith Fork of the Logan River is with a Mepps silver spinner?

Literally hundreds of state and local as well as national organizations exist that allow the sportsman to participate in a group and become educated about and lobby for not only the fish and game he harvests, but the synergistic elements as well, the elements on which the fish and game depend: the air, the water, the mountains, the forests.

Sitting out on the putting green, listening for the alligators, I ask myself for the hundredth time: would it not be easier to learn to dance? It is like this every time. I notice that the band is playing a slow song: I turn and look up at the clubhouse, and imagine that I see silhouetted against the big yellow window my date, slow-dancing with a burly good-looking rascal from Pascagoula. Surely it is my imagination. Anyway, it's my own fault. The dance ends, the band breaks up. Stiff and sorrowful at not hearing the alligators, I rise and go back to the clubhouse.

My date is laughing and gay when I get there: her eyes sparkle and gleam and she is playful—how she loves to dance! The fellow from Pascagoula is near her; I glower at him and he retreats into the crowd. We all drift out into the parking lot, rounding up rides back to Jackson so we can carpool, and we make sure the last one out turns off the lights. I pause at our car, open the door for my date, and then stand there, listening for a while, still listening for the gators, wishing Ocean Springs all the best and yet at the same time hoping that no matter how big it gets that at least some of the alligators will stay there for always, and then I walk around and get in the car and drive back to Jackson.

"Listen," said my date as I let her out at her house. "I had a wonderful time!"

I went home and fell asleep immediately and dreamed not of wood ducks and alligators but of house subcommittees and legislative battles waged over clean air and western wilderness areas.

3

On Camp Robbers, Rock Swifts, and Other Things Wild to the Heart

Friday, July 4, 1981

I've been waiting a long time for this. Jackson, Mississippi, is the best place for me to make a living, but there's this one small problem. There are no mountains. There aren't even any aspen.

The Pecos Wilderness Area, on the other hand, located fifteen beautiful miles up a winding canyon just west of the sleepy (and beautiful) little mountain town of Las Vegas, New Mexico, has plenty of both. That's why I'm here—to drink in the mountains and the aspen for a brief two-day Fourth of July vacation. I left Jackson at noon Thursday, after managing to talk the boss into letting me come into work early that day (4:00 A.M.) so I could have my eight hours in by noon. I'm due back in the office at nine o'clock Monday, but I could probably hold off till nine-fifteen and still sneak in without being labeled tardy, since everyone tends to linger in the coffee room a few extra minutes on Monday mornings. By driving straight through (both ways, averaging 54 mph. and stopping only for gas) it is an eighteen-hour drive each way, excluding the Texas-New-Mexico time change. (Much as I would like to, I can never bring myself to change my watch back when I cross over into it because it is too depressing to change it forward again when I come back out; someday I will, however, because someday I plan to cross over the line, pick up an extra hour, and never come back. Someday.)

Subtracting the thirty-six-hour round-trip drive from my ninety-three-and-a-quarter-hour allotment, this gives me exactly fifty-seven hours in the wilderness, in the mountains, in the aspen. My grand-parents live in Fort Worth, a rough geographical midpoint of the journey, and I usually call ahead both coming and going, and that is where I fritter away my extra quarter hour donated by the coffee-room congregation: seven-and-a-half minutes coming, and seven-and-a-half minutes going. It is inevitably right around midnight on the return trip, but they don't mind; they are waiting on the porch, waiting with a grocery sack full of out-of-this-world delicacies that grandmothers are famous for—sausage-and-biscuit sandwiches, slabs of angel food cake, pies, fresh peaches, brownies and cookies, barbe-cued ribs, and chicken still warm and wrapped in foil—and we hug, sit on the porch and talk about the weather, baseball, football, the upcoming hunting season, and then I leave. They too used to live in the mountains; they understand.

At any rate, it is now midafternoon; I got in around dawn this morning, being fortunate enough to reach the high open mountain meadows that stretch across the Great Divide along the deserted little one-lane road between Trujillo and Las Vegas just in time for sunrise, the most beautiful sunrise I've seen since my last three-day weekend. I stopped at the little donut store at the foot of the mountains in Las Vegas, the same one I always stop at—they're always fresh and hot at that time of the morning—grabbed a couple to go (one blueberry, one plain glazed) and headed up the canyon. Reached the Pecos Wilderness Area, turned down a dusty gravel road, headed uphill (my trusty VW bucked and pitched over the stones and cobbles but never faltered), stopped by a stream and a stand of aspen, got out, took a deep breath, then another and another, feeling, I suppose, like a man escaped from prison (surely someone must be chasing me; I half expected to hear hounds baying in the distance), put my hiking boots on, raised both arms high into the thin crisp mountain morning air and yelled as loud and as long as I could in one breath and then curled up in a ball on a cold flat rock down by the water's edge and slept for five hours solid, the deepest sleep I've had since, well, since my last three-day weekend.

After I woke I shouldered my pack, yawned, consulted my topo map, scarcely believing my luck—just yesterday I was in hot humid flat Mississippi!—and headed up a ridge toward where I hoped the trailhead to Hermit's Peak would be. The forested yet rocky mountain loomed in front of me like a barrier, about three miles distant, its east-facing sheer cliffs shining bright in the midday sun. The way to get up to the top is to sneak up the backside, up a gruelingly constant sixty-degree pitch of forested switchbacks and loop-arounds. Sometimes it is more of a climb than a hike, so that your hands grip rock ledges and pull you up the mountain instead of the conventional and more efficient feet-pushing-off-of-solid-ground style to reach the top. It is an enchantedly tortuous trail, through shady woods, past waterfalls and aspen, up and over talus slopes, through stream-fed mountain green meadows . . .

On my way up through the aspen I snack on the last of the sausage and biscuits (sweet madeleine!) and suddenly, all is well. Job pressures are gone, as are worries that I might never see aspen or feel the rough wild texture of the mountains on the palms of my hands again. I am back home again, for a couple of days anyway. The sausage and biscuit is always the real beginning of the best part of the trip; I always save one for this purpose. Everything before that last Grandmother's homemade biscuit is Getting There; everything afterward is There Itself.

I reach the trailhead a couple hours later, my muscles just now beginning to loosen to the pull of the pack the way they used to nearly every day, back before I had to start working for a living. Because it is the Fourth of July, there are a fair (or is it unfair?) number of people here, local people mostly, who have decided to make the all-day four-mile hike up and down the trail to the top of the magnificent windswept Hermit's Peak their Fourth of July celebration. Because I want the trail to myself, I try to dislike them for it, but cannot; if I lived in Las Vegas or Trujillo or Santa Fe or Carrizizo Springs it is what I too would do; it's what I'm doing anyway.

I've made the climb/hike before, but as I sit at the trailhead watching them come staggering down the trail in groups of twos and threes, staggering like mortally wounded buffaloes, tongues dragging and eyes crossing, a new herd every thirty minutes or so, I ask one of them what kind of hike it is, just to make conversation, just to make sure the mountain hasn't gotten taller.

One of the hikers (he left at dawn; it is now 3:00 P.M.; he is in shape) looks at my pack dubiously. Camera lenses, tripod, tent, sleeping bag, canteens and extra hiking boots (my old ones are threatening to go out any day now) spring out in all directions as if trying to escape.

"How much does your pack weigh?" he asks.

"Sixty pounds," I say. "I plan to stay a while."

He frowns, and I can tell that he is about to tell me that he doesn't think you can get to the top with a sixty-pound pack. "It took me six hours up," he says.

"Thank you," I say.

Glancing up at the sun, I figure there to be about five hours left before sundown; just right. I sit down by the Hermit's Creek and eat chocolate bars and listen to the water, and then, when it is four hours till sundown, four hours till alpenglow, after the last of the buffalo have filed past with wan and weary smiles, I start up the trail. No one else will be starting up behind me, and there is a good chance most of them will already have come down. I will have Hermit's Peak to myself. I don't know if that is what the Forest Service calls "multiple use" but it suits me just fine.

Friday, July 4, 1981, Later in the Evening

Up top. The two most delightful words in the world right now, because that is where I am: up top. There is no place else to go. It amazes me that my legs still work, but after a twenty-minute layover at Hermit's Spring—Marty Robbins was right: cool, clear, water!—I was able to make it up to the top, to the last meadow. Up top.

I'm just sitting here, savoring the complete and temporary ownership of the second-highest two hundred acres in New Mexico all to myself. It is really more of a small meadow plateau than a peak; it stands up in the clouds most of the time. I suffered a few minor bouts with altitude sickness on the way up, and my knees and hip joints are sufficiently weak and rusty enough to make the Tin Man's those of a spring chicken, but I am, Praise the Lord, Up Top, looking down on one of His better efforts, watching the alpenglow flush all of eastern New Mexico.

Gads, what's this? Voices from behind me, voices coming up the trail at sunset! Angels? Demons? Prophets? I turn to see two people, a man and a woman, striding eagerly up through the aspen; they are both thin, wiry, and tan, and the man has a golden blond beard. They are both wearing green nylon running shorts and white tee shirts that say "Property of Texas Tech University Track Team." They are not wearing backpacks. I look down at the sun (I am up top, up above it), or rather, where the sun used to be. Ten, maybe twenty minutes of light left; even I can be cordial for that long, I tell myself.

For a moment the crazy thought crosses my mind that if I were ninety years old and had a weathered white beard down to my knees I could charge out at them waving a staff and scream blue oaths and chase them back down the trail, thereby giving credibility to the legend that the hermit of Hermit's Peak does indeed exist, that he is living high up in a cave surviving on snakes and lizards and baby mountain goats, but instead I rise and take a step to meet them and offer them a chocolate bar. They certainly deserve it.

"Thanks," says the man, peeling back the wrapper without looking at it, his eyes glued to the dizzying sweep of endless forest far below, never blinking, never looking at anything else, as if he were watching the Second Coming. The girl smiles but shakes her head; she is, she tells me, on a diet.

"Wow," says the man, still watching the eastern United States as if waiting for something to happen. "I never thought it would be like this."

I smile proudly, as if it is some of my doing. "Pretty nice, huh?"

"Yeah," he says, sounding very distant and far off. "Pretty nice."

"It's gorgeous," says the girl.

We all three sit down and watch the wilderness below, just watching and waiting and eating chocolate bars, and then, after it is almost too dark to see, they sigh and look wistfully back at the trail behind us.

"We've really got to be going," says the man, like a dinner guest apologizing for leaving so early.

"We didn't bring our sleeping bags or anything," the girl says, shrugging her shoulders and pointing to her running shorts and track shirt as if I had just asked her for a light, or to make change for a dollar.

I smile benignly. "That's a shame," I say, almost managing to sound truly sorry. They nod glumly, look back out at the many-miles-distant now-darkened horizon one last time, and turn and start back down the trail. I turn and refocus my attention on the spot where the sun went down – a half dome of dull light blue glowing marks the point – and then, remembering my manners, pivot around again to tell them to be careful, but they are already gone, swallowed up. Maybe, I think wickedly and for no reason at all, maybe the hermit got them. I get up, pitch my tent by the light of a quarter moon, roll out my sleeping bag, stretch out on top of it, and fall fast asleep immediately, sleeping until nine o'clock the next morning.

Saturday, July 5, 1981

Right now there is a camp robber watching me from a distance of perhaps four, maybe five feet. If I had the mind to I think I could probably reach out and snatch him up before he even had a chance to think about flying away. He is just watching me, head cocked slightly, looking as if maybe he wants to come still closer. He's the first camp robber I've seen since reaching the summit; I am sitting out on the lip of a four-thousand-foot (almost a mile!) sheer cliff face and can see Texas and Colorado at the same time. It is too hazy to the south or I bet I could see Mexico too. I am facing east; behind me is the summit meadow in which I have pitched my tent and behind that is a forest of cool, green-leaved, white-barked aspen.

The ledge I'm sitting on is sloped so much that if I set a marble down on it, it would roll down the ledge a couple of yards before plunging over the edge and falling the four thousand feet down into the gorge below, disappearing into the morning haze long before it hits. The ledge is not so steep, however, that I can't sit on it with my feet out in front of me, relaxed, resting perhaps ten or twelve inches from the edge. My weight pressing down on the rock keeps me from sliding; I could probably even cross my feet, as in a lawn chair, and not have any trouble, but I think I will leave them uncrossed and ready for action, just in case I do start to slide. The camp robber could, for reasons unknown, suddenly rush at me, startling me, or there could be an earth tremor, or perhaps a sudden hurricane . . . it would be a shame not to be able to come back to this place.

The camp robber has hopped a step closer to me, not knowing that I do not plan to share my chocolate energy bar with him. Where was he when I was hauling it up the trail? Let him eat piñon nuts. We stare friendly, curious stares at each other for a moment and then he hops back a step, acquiescing. I can tell that there is no doubt in his mind that if he waits long enough, sooner or later I will give in and break off a square and toss it to him. He spreads his wings, shakes them, folds them again, and cocks his head, never taking his bright eyes from the bar, and waits.

Despite (or perhaps because of) their lack of glamour, camp robbers are the most ubiquitous wilderness bird I have come across; they are everywhere, like sparrows in the city. I think that if the truth were known, there are probably entire colonies of them living up on top of K2 and Everest and McKinley, only none of the climbers ever mention them in their diaries or logbooks because they are ashamed to.

I used to be ashamed to find camp robbers waiting for me when I got to the top of high wild windy peaks such as this one. Because camp robbers don't have a lot of romance about them. They are birds that make a living (whenever possible) by robbing crumbs from campers' picnic tables. Camp robbers are like the bears at Yellowstone who used to beg for food, only not as cute. Fluffy, midsized, non-descript, greyish looking birds with some slate-colored smudging of black on their wings and a handsome white puffed-out chest, they look a little like a chubby mockingbird.

The reason a lot of experienced and dedicated hikers and climbers choose to look upon camp robbers with no small amount of scorn, or at best, to ignore them, is because, to these experienced and dedicated hikers and climbers, camp robbers represent not wild windy peaks like the ones found in the Pecos Wilderness Area but instead remind them of mobile homes, Winnebagos, picnic tables, and Fourth of July family reunions down in the campgrounds. Roasting hot dogs and flaming marshmallows. Barking dogs and screaming children. Frisbees and firecrackers.

All of which are fine, but none of which is why the experienced and dedicated hikers and climbers came to the wilderness in the first place. So they hike and they climb and they hike and they climb and then they get to the top of Hermit's Peak or Wheeler's Peak or Crazy Elk

Mountain and they are disappointed to find that although they have escaped the suburbia of the campgrounds, they have not escaped the camp robbers.

There is merit in their disappointment. After a grueling all-day assault up the steep and rocky trail, after battling altitude sickness, blistered feet, pulled hamstrings and rubbed-raw-from-the-pack shoulders and backbones, it would be nice (in a quaint, egotistically human way) for them to be able to think that they have done something special, something a little grey bird cannot. But instead, just about the time they are leaning back against a juniper stump, feet stretched comfortably out in front of them, congratulating themselves, along hops the camp robber, begging for crumbs. To a lot of the experienced and dedicated ones, it is a real letdown. A hawk, perhaps, or maybe even an eagle, that would be all right, but a camp robber? They can almost taste the hot dogs.

I like camp robbers. I like them because they have some qualities I do not have but wish I did. They are extraordinarily friendly to everyone, whether they have to be or not. This is a pretty wild thought, due perhaps to yesterday's bout with altitude sickness, or maybe to the fact that I have been living on nothing but chocolate bars and fruit juice for the last couple of days, but I am convinced that if you could take a camp robber and turn him into high-school-aged youth, a boy, say, and send him to school for a week, then by the end of that week he would not only be elected Student Body President but would also be named Most Likely to Succeed, Most Representative Senior Boy, Most Handsome, and Most Popular. Because, except for the hikers and climbers who try to escape him, nearly everyone likes a camp robber. To most, they are cunning and clever and charming and smart. To me, they are friendly. I know of no other animal that shares such majestic wilderness so willingly, so completely, with man.

Take, for instance, this rock I am sitting on. The rock swifts who live below it are doing their level best to evict me. They have no hatchlings on their nests, no little ones, but they don't care: from time to time they fold their wings and dive straight out of the sun at me, wings tucked, before suddenly flaring out over the edge of the cliff and rocketing out into the haze, their trim bullet-shaped bodies ripping the air with the sound of tearing cloth, sometimes coming so close that if I had a net and if I was fast enough (fast enough to catch a bullet) I could reach out and net one. They are not amused by my presence. I have not littered, I have not hurled rocks at them as they fly past, I have not even played my harmonica late into the night, and yet, they do not like me. They feel toward me the way I felt toward the track couple last night – they will be glad when I leave. They want the Pecos Wilderness to themselves.

But not the camp robbers. They do not attack me, nor do they run and hide. They stay and sing and play childish games such as snatching up bits of chocolate I throw to them and then after I am gone they go back into the pines, back into the woods, and they still have their wilderness, still as wild and untouched as before, while their relatives the rock swifts continue to swoop and scream up and down the barren cliffs and rock faces, always on the lookout for more hikers and climbers against which they must defend their cliffs and rock walls. I feel sure there is a lesson in there somewhere but I am getting both sleepy and hungry at the same time, so I think I will return to my tent and eat a couple more chocolate bars, drink another can of apple juice, and then stretch out on a warm rock and doze off with only the sound of the wind and nothing else to think about.

Sunday, July 6, 1981

I believe I could tell today is a Sunday morning without even looking at a calendar; there is just something about them, even in the city, but, surprisingly enough, even more so in the mountains, that identifies them as a Sunday. Everything seems slower and more relaxed. This morning even my altitude sickness was gone; only the euphoria remained – a pleasant enough side effect. I slept with my tent flaps open so: (a) I could hear the night wind better; it will be Labor Day before I hear it again the way I heard it last night, and (b) so that the first faint light of sunup would wake me, which it did.

It was like a secret meeting, like an elopement. The sky began to lighten in the east around five A.M., and I got up and began moving around, wearing a light windbreaker and shorts and hiking boots – it was really much cooler than windbreaker-and-shorts weather, but I liked to feel the goose bumps – it would, I told myself, be another two months before I felt them again – and gathered up some wood for a small fire. There is a ton of dried windfall wood back on the south slope of Hermit's Peak; entire swaths of forest have been hit by lightning (in thunderstorms, the peak acts as the tallest lightning rod for many, many miles) and mowed down by windstorms of up to a hundred miles an hour. I spooked two elk on the southwest rim of the peak; they sounded like ten wild elephants as they crashed through the dead timber in their panic.

I gathered up two handfuls of kindling, came back to my tent, built a small fire on the edge of the four-thousand-foot face that looked out at the eastern U.S., and waited, shivering. Only it was better than a secret meeting, better than an elopement, because I knew for certain that the sun would be coming, that she would show up on time; I could already see her.

It took about an hour from first light until the first tiny flattened arc of orange fire peered up over the horizon, looking much larger than I had expected it would, but after the first arc appeared, the rest of the ball was not long at all in following; it rose as rapidly as if it were being pulled up by a string, like a stage curtain.

"Hello," I said, and for half a moment (was it the altitude sickness again?) I almost thought the sun was going to pause, but there was no reply, no time for a reply. She apparently had a busy day ahead of her, and continued to rise without acknowledging me. My fire dwindled; I poured water on the ashes, stirred them around, folded my tent, and broke camp. Headed down the trail, lingering, taking my time; it was still cold and dark on the backside of the peak, would be for another hour or so. Spooked another elk and got my camera out and took an especially crisp picture of the back of my lens cover. Stopped at Hermit's Spring again and ate a hard-as-ice cold candy bar – delicious! – and splashed water on my face. I suppose I could put a bowl of ice water in the refrigerator back in Jackson before going to bed each night and then splash some of it on my face first thing each morning, but somehow I just don't think it'd be the same. I got up from the rock I had been sitting on, yawned, stretched, and moved on, feeling both Sunday-morning-calm-and-peaceful but also euphoric – it must have been A.S., yes, surely that's what it was – and reached bottom, reached the trailhead, in time for lunch. The Fourth of July gang was long gone; only my little orange VW sat waiting patiently for my return, like a horse tied to a hitching post. I loaded my pack into the back seat and took my hiking boots off, wriggled my toes in the cold dust, put my soft old tennis shoes on, rubbed my three-days' beard for the first time, and sat on the hood of my car and ate more chocolate bars and looked up at Hermit's Peak for a while and waited for the euphoria to subside so I could leave. Down low in the campground the mountain air was thin and warm and tasted like Indian summer, like autumn in Mississippi.

I sighed; Mississippi. Mississippi on my mind. It could be postponed no longer; there were papers to be shuffled, reports to be filed, meetings to be attended, a living to be made. Sort of. I got in my car, turned the engine over, half hoping it wouldn't start, but it did, and I let the clutch out and drove slowly down the dusty gravel road into Las Vegas. Stopped for donuts in Las Vegas, gas in Tucumcari and Abilene, sausage and biscuits and barbecued ribs and hugs in Forth Worth, and gasoline again in Shreveport. Made good time, got into Jackson at eight-thirty Monday morning. Swung by the apartment and showered and changed, drove to the office (tied my tie, buckled my belt, put my shoes and socks on, and field-shaved at red lights), combed my hair in the elevator on the way up, and stepped out on the eleventh floor at 9:08 sharp. Paused at the office doorway before consulting my pocket calendar: sixty more days. I took a deep breath, straightened my tie, and stepped inside.

4

Good Day at Black Creek

YOU WOULD REALLY like Jim Trunzler, I know you would. In fact, it is hard to imagine anyone not liking him; the thought of someone frowning when his name is mentioned, or—get this!—of someone calling him a name in anger is so unimaginable that it is ludicrous. He is just one of those types. Ask someone who knows him to describe him to you and inevitably the description will begin with a chuckle-chuckle or a heh, heh. In his younger days, Jim used to be a bit of a card. A rather large bit of one. He will be thirty-eight years old this January first.

He looks like a big gnome. He has curly red hair and a wild red beard and eyes that are ever twinkling, as if he had just ducked around the corner after playing a massive practical joke on somebody;

many times this is precisely the case. He smokes a pipe and has large beefy shoulders and thick strong biceps. He is a foreign car mechanic and an avid whitewater kayaker-canoer. He is chairman of the Central Mississippi Sierra Club and he invited me to go backpacking with him one day while I was in his shop having my car worked on. I had never met him before.

"I'd love to," I said. "When are you going?"

"Tomorrow morning."

"I'll be there."

There are ten of us going, I discover; Jim mills around, talking with everyone before we leave, offering them coffee, disgruntled when they defer, ecstatic when they accept. Not knowing about his coffee, I make the mistake of falling into the acceptor category. I taste it, make a face, and when he is not looking, pour it out in the street. It tastes like india ink.

Packs are transferred to the cars that will be making the trip. Tires are thumped, hoods checked, and windshields cleaned. Jim's slender black cat, Ender, watches from under a hedge; all we can see of him is wide wondering eyes as round as saucers and as green as limes, looking at us as if he cannot, for some reason, believe what he is seeing. We try to coax him out to come with us, but it is no go; he is too smart. We get in the cars and wave good-bye to him. I have, luck of all lucks, managed to be in Jim's car. He has an ancient golden Volvo that he has rebuilt himself. It has a fantastic radio-cassette system, worth easily as much as the car itself. The morning sky is blue and crisp and cloudless: it is mid-February and a good morning for driving. We crack the windows a bit to let the cold fresh air whirl around, and the sweet melodic strains of James Taylor fill the air. He is singing a song about going to Carolina in his mind. It is mountain music; it is good music. For the first time I think to ask Jim where we are going to backpack. Black Creek, he tells me.

Located about 120 miles south of Jackson, about 50 miles north of the Gulf of Mexico, the Black Creek Wilderness Area is not yet officially a real wilderness area, not a designated one anyway, but it is trying to be. If approved and accepted into the National Wilderness Preservation system as was originally suggested by the Roadless Area Review & Evaluation program (RARE II), it will become Mississippi's first and only national wilderness area. The Black Creek wilderness is comprised of thousands of acres of swamps, hills, valleys, meadows, ridges, hardwood bottoms, and pine plantations through which the wide and deep and dark and cool Black Creek wanders, heading south, south to the Big Water. Broad-leaved cottonwoods and great thick sycamores line the banks of the river; the water is rich and golden black, tangy with the taste of fallen acorn tannin, and out in the still pools, behind the riffles and log jams, sulk great bull-headed catfish. Bullfrogs as big as waste baskets sit like green boulders on the banks and drum in the summertime; at dusk, cautious deer and bold raccoons can be seen coming right down to the crystal white sandbars that bound the meandering river. Bobcats pad silently through the leaves, stalking terrified, prolific cottontails, and red-tailed hawks wheel overhead in lazy figure eights. Some of the scattered handfuls of farmers who live near the borders of the proposed wilderness area swear they have heard mountain lions screaming back in the swamps; one man says he saw a bear. The Black Creek region, Jim tells us, is the wildest, most unspoiled land in the entire state; if indeed there are black bears remaining in Mississippi, Black Creek is almost certainly where they will be holed up.

We pass through Hattiesburg an hour and a half later; we begin to stir. A peppy, springy pop tune by Emmylou Harris is playing, and Jim drums his hands on the steering wheel—I noticed later that he seems to be happiest when he is moving, whether he is in a car, in a kayak, or even just walking—and he asks Curt, his copilot, to please pour him another cup of that delicious coffee from the thermos stashed on the floorboard. Curt obliges; there is plenty left. Curt pours while Jim steers with one hand and holds the cup with the other, watching the road nervously. Looking for excitement, cramped and restless after ninety minutes of riding, I lean forward, waiting for the car to hit a bump and make Curt pour it in Jim's lap, but it doesn't, and I sit back, disappointed. Thank you, says Jim. Curt says that it is nothing. It is Mardi Gras weekend in New Orleans, and the interstate is deserted: we are the only car on the road.

We exit the interstate and drive down a bumpy two-lane back-country road until we reach a sleepy little crossroads town with the unlikely name of Brooklyn, where we pull into a gravel parking lot and wait for Ron Fralik, who is supposed to be coming up from the coast to meet us there.

With a population of almost a thousand, Brooklyn is the last civilization before entering the Black Creek Wilderness Area, and at 10:00 A.M. on this sunny February morning it is awhirl with activity. A pale, long-legged, houndish dog walks down a side street, casting glances from side to side at all the stores. Farther down the road, a boy on a three-wheeler races figure eights around two oak trees in someone's front yard. Roosters are crowing somewhere; the flag over the post office hangs motionless. I go in the little store whose parking lot we are parked in—there is a screen door; a bell jingles when I enter—and buy a pint of chocolate milk and a moon pie. The girl at the counter gives me six cents too much change, and I can tell that it is going to be a beautiful day.

We gather around the cars, sitting on bumpers and hoods, and drink our chocolate milks and Mountain Dews and Bubbly-Fizz root beers and watch the boy down the street on the three-wheeler for a while, glancing occasionally at the sun or at our watches. Late ourselves, we were supposed to have met Ron at the store between nine-thirty and ten o'clock; it is now ten minutes after. Susan Haskins begins a series of stretching exercises that culminates in her placing one foot up on top of Louis McCool's pickup, the roof of which is taller than she is, and touching her head to her knee: we are all properly amazed. We glance at our watches again. The sun is warm, the day pretty; we wait four minutes and then leave.

"He knows where to find us," says Jim.

But do we know where to find him? We are supposed to catch the trail at a remote backwoods crossing called Janice Landing. We miss the turn: we find ourselves on a red gravel road that noses up and down steep pine-studded ridges, carrying us past greying farm shacks and collapsing chicken coops. Ancient tractors sit quietly abandoned in the small stumpy fields, overcome at last by time and rust; we are lost, but at least it is pretty. The road winds and loops and bends back and forth through the forest, so that each corner brings something new. The sun is warm, it is like summertime in February. We leave a cloud of swirling red dust behind us wherever we go and must roll up the windows. The Volvo climbs hills easily; the woods slide by.

We reach the top of a ridge and look down on the road we are supposed to be on. We turn around and head back down the road we just came up, looking for a turn-off. Jim begins to draw harder and faster on his cigarette. Gears clash sometimes now when he shifts, and surprised chickens squawk and cluck angrily and scatter to either side of the road as we blow past them again, anxious to be back on the trail. We find it twenty minutes later. Jim smiles, appeased now, and we unload the cars and lock up.

Black Creek is a different sort of wilderness from what most people are used to. It is not as remote as the sprawling thousand-square-mile chains of mountain spurs and subranges up in the Rockies, nor is it as isolated as the deserts of the Southwest. It is a buffered sort of wilderness. It is not Precambrian virginal, not like a peak up above treeline a hundred miles from even the nearest mining camp out West, but rather, it is an 1800s sort of wilderness: it is probably as close as is possible to being identical to what the country's first settlers encountered when they ventured into the southeastern hardwood bottoms two hundred years ago, when there were only brief, short-lived, and thinly populated little fishing camps, little trading posts, and little settlements scattered throughout the South: Rabun Gap, Georgia; Smoke Holler, Alabama; Janice Landing, Mississippi . . . It is not wilderness in the sense that it is five hundred miles from a telephone or a hard-topped road or a farm with running water and electricity, but it is wilderness in the sense that it has never been wilder, that this is how it was and always has been, even in prehistoric food-gathering-tribal times. Small, even tiny patches of the great forest are frequently cut over and harvested for management purposes, but again, this is how it has been since the country's beginnings: settlers felling logs for cabins, and clearing tiny openings deep in the thick forest depths for subsistence farming. At night, camped on a sandbar, you can still hear hounds running coons far away, running through the swamp bottoms all night long, and it is possible to imagine their men sitting up on a knoll around a small fire, telling stories and listening to their dogs, waiting for the right kind of bay, the right kind of frenzied *awoooooh!* that will tell them they've found one, so they can snatch up their guns and kerosene lanterns and go hurrying off through the bottoms in the direction of the dogs, stumbling over logs, clawing briars and vines out of the way . . .

It is not wilderness in the sense that other people, such as the coon hunters, never venture into it, but it is wilderness in the sense that it is still wild, and in the sense that it is unchanged: that it is, essentially, as it always has been.

On the trail I follow Jim so I can smell his pipe smoke. It is cherry scented; it is delicious. It fills the entire woods with a gruff yet mild benign aura; it makes the woods seem even friendlier, and it relaxes me. It is mellow. I myself do not smoke because it cuts down on my wind.

Hiking behind Jim, I shift and jiggle my pack; it feels good to be carrying a pack through the woods on a warm winter day; it feels good to have all I need on my back. Ahead of us both trudges sturdy Ron Fralik with calves like diamonds; he climbs hills as does the Volvo – effortlessly. After a while I notice that Jim's pack is getting smaller and smaller; I hurry to catch up.

I watch for armadillos as I go. Not found in Mississippi ten years ago, they are now fairly common in the Black Creek wilderness, having migrated up from Mexico and into Texas around the turn of the nineteenth century, spilling slowly northward ever since then, and Jim has offered a five-dollar reward to anyone who can catch one before dinner. Originally from Texas himself, Jim claims they are not only edible, but tasty. We do not know if he is joking or not, but we keep a watch anyway.

We stop and have lunch on a tall vertical bluff looking straight down into Black Creek. White wine, Swiss cheese, California golden raisins, dried apricots and sardines and apples and stone-ground wheat crackers – I am impressed. I chew thoughtfully on my squashed peanut butter and jelly sandwich and think to myself that next time I will have to do better: this crowd travels in style. I take a sip of warm water from my canteen and lean back against a thick-trunked white oak and close my eyes and doze. Peanut butter and jelly sandwiches almost always make me sleepy, and especially so on warm afternoons in the woods in February. I notice that everyone else is doing the same, even though they have not had the p b and j. Perhaps it is something in the air: it settles over us like a net, like a malaise, only it is pleasant. No one says anything; everyone dozes and listens to the woods. It is a group that believes firmly in proper digestion; it is a group after my own heart.

Dozing, it strikes me that if another group of hikers were to come trudging up the trail and find us leaning against trees like this, they would think we had all been poisoned, and I smile lazily without opening my eyes. Down in a creek branch somewhere below us, a blue jay scolds; out on the river, two wood ducks squeal as they rocket down its length. I have always believed in proper digestion.

An hour later we are hiking again, roaring up and down the trails as if the woods are on fire. These bearded Southerners with their long loping strides are leaving me fast behind. I am not originally from Mississippi. I am from northern Utah, where it begins snowing up above treeline in late August and where the backpacking trails often hug skylines so high that the air turns purple, almost black, and the wind blows hard and strong twelve months out of the year, and where a three-mile hike is often a day's work, and all uphill. Different muscles are used, and a different pace: different physiologies are developed. Rocky Mountain backpackers are often short and squatty, like tanks.

But tanks do not fare well in the delta woodlands; I practice unlearning my short, shuffling, power-climbing steps and try to smooth them out into steady and rhythmic ground-eating ones, and by the end of the day, I am beginning to get the hang of it.

We camp, of course, on the river, on a white sandbar. Firewood is gathered, and tents are pitched; dusk descends like a grey curtain. Owls boom, and bats chitter and swoop overhead, darting across the river, always altering their flights at the last microsecond to swerve and snap at some invisible insect. A fish breaks water out on the river, but there are no mosquitoes; it is still too cool, too crisp.

Half disappointed and half relieved that no armadillos were sighted, we all cook on the one big community fire, comparing recipes and dinners. Tim has four servings of spaghetti, three more than he needs, and we all sample it; Larry has brought too many hot dogs and distributes them freely. Coleman is on a diet, and plays his harmonica. Louis and Susan, to be married in June, walk off down the river holding hands: we tell Susan to watch out for bears.

"And panthers," calls out Jim.

"And alligators," says Curt.

Susan hesitates and moves in a little closer to Louis and looks back and then relaxes. Surely we are kidding. An owl booms again, and then they disappear around a bend in the river.

Because none of us really knew each other, there had not been a lot of talking on the trail this first day. Jim had led a blistering (literally) pace; whether he did this on purpose or not, I do not know, but that night we are all much closer, much more sociable and relaxed as we sit around the fire in varying states of shared exhaustion, massaging our feet and making up names for different stars. Jim sits back away from us and puffs benignly on his pipe and tells funny jokes from time to time. The sweet sure scent of cherry pipe smoke fills the night woods. We watch the fire and talk about everything. Louis and Susan return, and they too come over and sit down with us and watch the fire, and then, sure enough, we hear dogs. So for an hour or so we listen to them. They sound wild; they sound happy.

After a while, Jim says, "I believe one of them is coming this way." It is true: one of the barks is growing louder.

"It sounds like he's on the other side of the creek," says Larry.

After a while the baying stops.

"That'll be him crossing the creek," Larry says casually. Susan edges closer to Louis and asks if perhaps we shouldn't douse the fire.

"What if he chases whatever it is he's chasing right through camp?" she asks, somewhat fearfully.

"Maybe it'll be an armadillo," Jim says hopefully. The baying starts up again.

"That'll be him on our side of the creek, coming towards us now," Larry tells her.

Soon we can hear the rustling of leaves and crash of vines as he scrambles up the ravine toward us; he is no longer barking. Sitting around the fire, our eyes straining into the darkness, we all—except for Susan—know it is just an old stray hound mistaking our fire for his owner's, but still, forgotten pre-Neanderthal genes stir uneasily within us, and we squint out into the blackness. The rustling stops, and we can hear him standing there, panting. Coleman flicks on a flashlight and shines it into the woods, and two fiery red orbs gaze back at us.

"What a beast," Jeff marvels.

"Look at his legs," Larry whispers.

"C'm here, boy," Jim whistles. The dog slinks forward, wagging his tail ecstatically, delighted to be taking this brief respite from the hunt, unbeknownst to his master. Off in the woods, maybe three or four miles away, we can barely hear the rest of the pack, headed in what sounds to be the opposite direction.

The dog heads straight for Larry. He must know that Larry still has a leftover hot dog. Larry feeds it to him; the dog snaps it up. We shine a flashlight on his collar and discover that his name is Vernon Mitchell and that he lives in Wiggins, Mississippi. The fire dies and the coals flicker: we watch them until they too are gone, and then we go to bed, with Vernon Mitchell lying outside Larry's tent, standing guard, dreaming simple dog dreams of unexpected but delicious frankfurters doled out by total strangers in the middle of the night deep in the Mississippi wilderness.

Lazy Sunday mornings, both sunny and smoky-steamy with burning-off fog, are when Black Creek is at its best. Summer afternoons in the deep cool swimming holes are almost as fun, and evenings are beautiful too, but the difference between morning and evening is the difference between a beautiful smiling woman and a beautiful angry one. The mornings are the smilers; gentler than the evenings, they are sun dappled and refreshing, and offer up great hope for the day no matter what yesterday was like.

This lazy Sunday morning is no different; amidst Jim's exhortations to "get vertical," we are off, plodding along our southeasterly course a good two hours before the crack of noon. Vernon follows.

We get lost right from the start. It is our own fault; we flush a wild turkey scratching in the sand in the middle of the trail and take the wrong fork, the unmarked one, watching where he has flown instead of where we should be going, and after fifteen minutes we realize we have stopped seeing the small white blazes marked on trees every one hundred yards that characterized the other trail. We are lost.

The rest is welcome; we sit down in the warm sun and close our eyes. Jim consults his map and tries to look worried. Ron and Coleman take off in opposite directions, looking for the white blazes; Tim and Curt go back down the trail to see if we missed a turn-off. Jim studies his map a little more, and lights up his pipe; smoke rises. Jeff and Larry begin humming the theme from "The Twilight Zone."

"We need to backtrack," Jim says finally, and rolls up his map and stuffs it in his pack and waits for the others to return. Ron and Coleman come trotting back in, luckless, but Tim and Curt come back up the trail and inform us that we need to backtrack.

Back on the trail again, we jump a big buck deer, and Vernon starts off in glorious pursuit, but with sharp, indignant cries we call him back: does he not know it is Sunday? Incredulous, he gives up the chase and returns, sulking, glowering even, and contents himself with casting back and forth across the trail for rabbit scents.

Sunday's pace is more leisurely. We drink from fast-running streams, and watch for armadillos again, and try to identify bird calls; lunch, held in a grassy meadow, once again makes allowances for proper digestion. We reach the cars around midafternoon, our feet sore but our spirits stronger than when we came; we are ready once more to face the rigors of Jackson. We wave good-bye to Vernon and then load our packs in the trunks and get in the cars and drive off. He stands back in the woods and watches us leave and then turns and pads on back down the trail, back toward Wiggins. There is no telling what he was thinking.

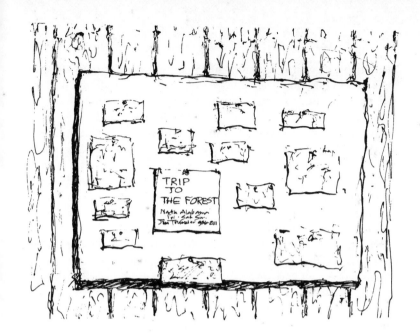

5

Sipsey in the Rain

I'M SUPPOSED TO meet Jim Trunzler and the Mississippi Sierra Club in the Bankhead National Forest Friday night. They're leaving from Jackson, a five-hour drive. I'm leaving from Tuscaloosa; I was in a business meeting all day, so I'm already halfway there. I don't know who'll get there first. They have farther to drive, but they've been there before: they know the way. This will be my first trip.

I didn't know you could backpack in the South. I thought you had to go out West, to Colorado or even Montana, or at least to north Georgia, to the Appalachian Trail. When I saw on a bulletin board in my office building where Jim and Co. were going to lead a trip to this Bankhead area (north of Birmingham), I called him up; I met him for lunch. He drew me a map on the back of a napkin. He told me to meet them there around midnight Friday. He asked if I was afraid of owls. I told him no.

Also, I did this: I lost the napkin.

Steering with my knees—it is dusk, and I am driving through the North Alabama mountains of Nowhere (last town was Samantha, pop. 27)—I unfold my eastern United States road map and squint. My car's interior dome light is out, so I have to hold a penlight in my teeth to see. I drive slowly; I look up and check the road as I drive, but there is no traffic out. Why I don't pull over and look at the map sitting still I don't know.

Yes I do know—it's because I'm in a hurry. It would be a real feather in my cap to find a good backpacking place this close to home. I grew up out West, and have discovered that if I go more than three weeks without a camping trip, my left eyebrow begins to twitch. A month, and my stomach makes funny noises in public. Five weeks and I drool and sometimes babble incoherently and without warning feeble poetry about mountain larkspurs and aspen.

I've never found out what happens after six weeks.

So I'm in a hurry. Eager. Hopeful. I discover that I'm holding the map upside down, and readjust it accordingly. With the blunt end of an index finger that looks enormous as it traces the thin red skein of County Road 13, I trace my way up to the Bankhead National Forest.

The Sipsey Wilderness Area lies along the northern boundaries of the forest and is outlined in green; it looks like my best bet will be to go north up through Haleyville and then turn into the forest at Rabbit Town. I put the map down, clear my throat, and accelerate.

I saved at least thirty seconds.

A bridge. I seem to remember something about a bridge. It clatters under me as I roll slowly across it; it is old and wooden, and below me I can hear the fast hard gurgle of a creek. It's dark out, but it sounds like a big creek. Faintly, I seem to remember something about a creek too. I wish I still had the napkin. A deer runs across the road (buck? doe? I cannot tell; it is the weekend after Easter; it is April 17) and I tap my brakes and beep my horn, but the horn doesn't work.

First the interior dome light, and now the horn. They both worked when I left Tuscaloosa. Perhaps the Sipsey Wilderness Area is consuming my automobile, bit by bit. Another deer runs across the road, and another, and another. Perhaps the woods are on fire; perhaps Jim and Co. are here and are running through the woods chasing the deer.

No, they're not, because no one is here. It's only seven o'clock, but it's as black as a licorice jelly bean, and chilly. Nice, but crisp. It is fun to go places in the spring where I've never been before. There's no one here; I'm all alone. I've not even seen a beer can on the road.

The road. It's gravel, sometimes mud. I seem to have been on it for quite some time. Little rocks and pebbles *chink!* up all around me. I'm driving with the windows down, driving very slowly. I pass through a creek bottom hollow, and an owl booms, surprisingly close.

I seem to remember something about a hollow, too, a hollow by the bridge—was that where they were going to camp Friday night?— and I start to stop, but the owl booms again. I roll the windows up and keep driving.

The stars are out, the night is clear. The forecast is rain, but they're mistaken. I drive to the top of a ridge, pull off to the side, park, get out, and hike across some slickrock and into a grassy little meadow. To the west, the far-off drums of thunder are ominous, but it will not rain; I can see the stars. I set my tent up and then light my propane lantern and sit outside and read for a while. It is nice out, too cool for mosquitoes. I read for almost an hour before the rain chases me in. There is thunder, there is lightning.

I wake up once during the night, but the tent is dry. I go back to sleep.

Morning. Still raining. I lie on my back and listen to it *pit!* against the tent before remembering I left my breakfast squares in the car. I pull on my boots and crouch like a sprinter and bolt for the car, but once outside I'm surprised to find it's only misting.

When you're closed in a tent, it always sounds like it's raining harder than it really is.

Delighted at this good fortune, I dance out across the pine straw, turn a whirl, jump up and down, and do a little dance, sort of a stamp-stamp-stamping dance.

I would not have done it if anyone had been watching. It felt good to be in the woods again. I sat on a rock and ate two blueberry energy bars.

Hint: if you are ever driving out of your campsite on a Saturday morning on your way to meet some other people and you do something really dumb like not watch where you are going, so that you drive off the road and get stuck in the mud, then you will do well to remember that the only way to get out is to jack the car up and put rocks and logs under the wheels.

Do not ask me how I know this, I just know.

After I got the car unstuck, I was pretty muddy, so I went back up in the woods and stripped down and stood there in the mist and toweled off with my tee shirt and then real quickly put some clean dry clothes on. It felt good; it was like a shower without a shower curtain.

I would not have done that either if anyone had been watching. I ran back down the hill feeling refreshed and clean, running fast so I would not get wet. It felt good to run so fast.

It was a good morning.

I found Jim and Co. by the smell of Jim's cherry pipe smoke. They were breaking camp; they were wearing rain gear, and cooking under a fly. They looked happy too—no eyebrow tics or growling stomachs this weekend. I noticed that none of them were eating blueberry energy bars however, and I felt guilty. I wondered how they had gotten their fire started with wet firewood.

There are two basic philosophies concerning the preparation and consumption of food on a backpacking trip. The first, and most glamorous, is to spend a week or so beforehand dawdling over cookbooks and mulling through grocery stores, picking up spices and cheese graters and odds and ends and knickknacks, and then planning a very detailed, very elegant menu.

In camp, spend a lot of time preparing it, spend even more time cooking it, eat it slowly, and then sit back and smoke a cherry pipe and rest easy for a while before cleaning up all your utensils. Total time: two hours, forty-eight minutes.

Or, you can do this: cram your pack with blueberry energy bars and raisins and Vienna sausages. Total time: twelve minutes.

Some people eat better when they are camping, some eat worse.

I sat under the fly with them and waited for them to finish cooking and eating and cleaning up. They kept offering me food; I kept telling them I had already eaten.

I began to consider changing philosophies.

Jim introduced me to everyone. I tried to remember their names as they told them to me. Jim's hiking partner was Eck. "Eck?" I said. "Eck." she nodded. "Like the sound a frog makes," she said. She did not explain what it stood for, or what her real name was—that might have been it—and I did not ask. She was four feet, eight inches tall.

Another guy had a moustache, and another a beard. One girl had on a bright new blue rain suit. There were seven of us.

We put in at a place called Bee Branch, up on a ridge. The plan called for us to go down the ridge toward Thompson Creek—more of a river, really, especially today—and follow it for a dozen or so miles before coming out of the woods at the Thompson Creek Bridge, where we had left one of the cars.

On the trail, we talk and surge and shift and chatter; our packs are heavy, and it is still misting, but we are dry, and our stomachs are full. It is cool; there is a frost warning for that night. Fat white dogwood petals float like snow out over the creek on the ends of slender limbs; viewed from a distance, the limbs are invisible, so that the petals look suspended in midair. It is beautiful.

Everyone wears ponchos. I ask the girl in the blue rain suit ahead of me what her name is and she tells me it is Sue. The trail drops steeply.

Suddenly, we are in a canyon. I am beside myself with joy. Slick rock walls, sheer faces, wet with leaking springs; tall cliffs, like out West! There are dogwoods everywhere: the blossoms hang motionless over the canyon, and our boots fall silently on the thick carpet of fern and moss. There are huge leafy trees everywhere; it is like a drizzling rain forest. Thompson Creek sounds wild. There are felt-covered green boulders everywhere, the smallest ones as big as refrigerators, and we pick our way around them.

The lure of the creek is irresistible. We will not stop until we get there.

We pass a tree bigger than the rest and pause to marvel at it. Five of us ring it and try to encircle it by holding hands, but cannot; a sixth is needed, and then a seventh. We cheer when we link up, though; we have it trapped. We stand there a moment and listen to it grow. Bill, the guy with the moustache, remarks that this tree is probably older than all of us put together. We look up at the top, or at least as high as we can see, and the understatement of his guess makes us all dizzy.

There are some big trees down in the creek bottoms of the Sipsey

Wilderness Area. We argue a while before finally deciding that this one will be 1017 years old this June fifth. We all agree that it would make a very loud noise if it ever fell: Doc (the guy with the beard) says that it would probably rattle windows in Birmingham and cause power outages in Atlanta.

May the woods never hear such a noise.

We reach the creek. It is like a rain forest; it is still raining lightly, but we are used to it—it is mystical. The moss-covered canyon walls box us in; a waterfall spouts over the top and showers down into the creek. It is a big waterfall; a rainbow spray mist surrounds the waterfall for many yards.

We sit on boulders and snack on peanut butter on wheat crackers and dried coconut and banana chips and watch the mist stipple the river. I look back up at the big tree and become dizzy again. It is centuries older than we. Castles were built over in Scotland, grew old and rotted and fell to the ground as it was growing. Growing a little bigger each year.

Deer that have been dead three hundred years had passed under its boughs.

Had anyone suspected, when they first saw it as a seedling, that it would ever get that big?

Had there ever been anyone to see it as a seedling in the first place?

There are no paintings, no hieroglyphics on the wall to indicate tribal civilizations. Either that, or the rain washed them off. It rains a lot in the Bankhead National Forest in April. Bring a poncho, or a blue rain suit.

A turkey gobbles, just once, and far off: we all look at one another happily, as if we had been given a gift—a real turkey gobble! At ten-thirty in the rain!

Surely it is going to be a very good day.

A green-and-yellow frog spooks and springs out of some ferns—bounds once, twice, three times—and then he is in the river and we all look at Eck: he called her name before jumping. Eck giggles. We rise, and move on.

I am in the lead; a raccoon trundles across the path in front of me, scolding at the mist. I am beside myself. I am the only one who sees it.

We stop for lunch a few hours later; these Jackson folks are an eating crowd. It's still raining, still misting. We've all got rain gear, though, and our packs are dry: the rain might as well give up and go away. I look all around me as we rest. Everywhere, great sprawling roots of unidentifiable trees clutch the green felt boulders like angry fingers; they are literally growing out of the rocks. It's amazing; it's like a hidden world, where nature does things you've never seen.

More hiking later on. We come to a side creek that can only be described as "swollen." It looks angry; it looks in pain. It makes a loud rushing sound at us as we stand on its banks. It tells us to go away.

A slender tree has been felled across it. The tree is green and limber, and slick with rain; it is barely wider than a man's foot. There's nothing to hold on to, either—no hand rails. The side creek is perhaps twenty feet wide at this point, but it is obviously the only place to cross. Jim takes his boots and socks off and tightropes across. No problem.

Jim was a member of the 1964 U.S. Olympic Gymnastic Team. He stops and lights his pipe and then does a little dance when he gets out over the middle of the creek. He bows; he does another little kick-dance, the kind the Russian vodka dancers do on top of tables. We are not amused. The women talk of turning back. I try to pretend that is a silly thing to consider; I try to pretend that I'm not glad they're suggesting it. I wonder to myself if we all closed our eyes and wished on the count of three, whether or not we could make Jim's sapling break. He's left his pack on shore; he's trying it out without the pack first, for safety's sake. He's thirty-seven years old; he should be ashamed of himself.

In the end, we form a sort of conveyer belt. All the guys line up across the log, straddle-legged—one foot facing east, one west—and pass everyone's packs down the line. Then we all walk gingerly and shakily to the other side.

It is the ladies' turn now. They go one at a time, with a rope tied around their waists; we hold the rope and watch, nervous ourselves.

Jane goes last. Jane cannot swim. We are extra nervous with Jane. She doesn't fall in, though, and we all cheer when she is across. We shoulder our packs and look back at the big creek and marvel for a moment; it is the first time a lot of us have done anything like that. One minute we were on one side, and then we were on the other. Just like that.

Feeling coltish and giddy with leftover excitement, we start up the steep hill. "That was fun," says Eck. I look at her carefully to see if she is being sarcastic, but I swear I don't think she was. But then you could expect as much from a girl named Eck.

It stops raining shortly before dark, as we are making camp for the night. I say making camp; what camp really consisted of was this: unrolling our sleeping bags under the overhang of the Big Cave.

It's probably got a name locally–Throne Room of the Gods, or Thunder Palace, or something like that–but for us, it was the Big Cave.

It was big enough to sleep a dozen, easily.

We were the only ones in the cave that night; north of that swollen creek, we were the only ones in the entire Wilderness Area. We began casting about for semi-dry twigs and branches. It was a challenge.

We get the fire going. It cheers us even more than we already are. Though it is still daylight, a bottle of white wine is produced. Dusk hangs over the river below in a quiet, satisfied mist; bats and night birds chatter and swoop across its surface with great energy, with great excitement.

Jim is a foreign car specialist; Doc is a neurosurgeon. Jane is an architect, and Eck's a schoolteacher. We sit with our feet dangling over the cliff and pass the bottle like bums. It's fun. We stand up and take turns trying to imitate the little dance Jim did on the log this afternoon. We sit back down and watch the river, and watch the night come in. We go back to the fire and add more wood to it. It blazes; it lights up the cave. We grow more cheerful still.

Jim cooks pizza for all of us; it's his surprise. He has, he tells us, brought seven different kinds of cheese. He busies us all with the preparations: mixing dough, grating cheese, cracking eggs. I am instructed to slice the eggplant.

There is (as there is in all of us) a small streak of the bizarre in Jim Trunzler. It needs letting out every now and then; it needs a release of the tension. I politely chose to view this abnormality of bringing eggplant pizza as a minor illness, and (politely) avoided mentioning it to him. I washed my hands in the little waterfall that spattered down off the cliff above us; I sliced the eggplant.

Baking in the fire, in foil, it smelled good. He cooked it for thirty minutes.

Is it possible for someone to go twenty-four years under the mistaken impression that he doesn't like eggplant?

Yes.

After the eggplant there were jokes, of course. We laughed; we talked. The fire faded, and we yawned. The river's cadence pitched and changed occasionally: changing water loads from the day's numerous earlier rainfalls did this. There were no sounds other than the river; we were too close. There were no stars either; there were too many trees around to see the sky.

No one had a watch. We went to bed. It could have been eight-thirty, or it could have been a quarter past one.

What did it matter?

Breakfast, and some of us are back on the ledge, watching the sun come up. We're discussing those two philosophies I talked about earlier, the ones about cooking. Behind us, Jim is cooking blueberry pancakes: we can smell the blueberries. I open another can of Vienna sausages and drain the oil over the edge of the cliff.

But my spartan breakfast leaves me free to do this: while everyone else is cleaning up, while they are still cooking even, I get my pack all ready to go and then leave it in the cave and wander down the talus slope, down to the river. The sun's up pretty good now; it's a warm Sunday morning, not bad at all for the week after Easter. I sit on the rocks in my shorts and a tee shirt and read a paperback about a cattle rancher in Montana. There's a little breeze; the river music is relaxing too, and slowly, I move through the chapters.

Again, no watch. Perhaps I read for fifteen minutes; perhaps two hours.

I'm not sure why I looked up, or how long he'd been sitting there watching me. I think I was in his spot, or where he wanted to be; I was in the brightest, warmest patch of sunlight on the entire talus slope. I recognized him immediately as a patch-nosed garter snake. He noticed me looking at him, and flicked his tongue, and then – I swear I am not making this up, he really did this – looked embarrassed. He turned and slithered in and out of some rocks, down into some brush.

A butterfly comes sailing by ninety-to-nothing, a black-and-yellow barred one, comes sailing across the spot where that snake sat coiled not twenty seconds ago. I am awed at the workings of this event: it is like Fate showing off. I like butterflies, I like them a lot, and yet I find myself wanting to cry out to the snake, "Wait! Come back! if only you had waited a little longer . . ."

The butterfly breezes past, never even slows down.

I refocus; I am startled to see the snake again, just a little farther down the slope. He hasn't left after all; he's watching the swallowtail. I can tell he's watching it because his tongue is not flicking. He's got it folded back in against the roof of his mouth, and he's just sitting there, spellbound, thinking about how good that particular kind of butterfly tastes. The butterfly flits, dips, pauses at a flower, then glides toward the snake.

I can see it coming before it happens. Awed and aghast, I shout a warning, but they ignore me: they rise toward each other like friends, the butterfly drifting and the snake striking.

The snake misses. (I like to think it was my yell that threw him off.) The butterfly leaps higher into the air, terrified, and careers off crazily into the woods. The snake coils back, tests the air again with his tongue, glares at the spot where the butterfly was a second ago, and then races off into the woods himself.

Embarrassed again, no doubt.

Eck comes down to the creek to see what I was shouting at. "A bear," I tell her. She turns and runs back up to the camp.

But really, there might be bears in the Sipsey after all; who knows? It's a wilderness area; it's wild. Last night I dreamed of bears.

Are there bears in the Sipsey? Is it truly that wild, that free?

I don't know, but I do know this: one time I dreamed of a friend I hadn't seen in over ten years, a friend I didn't even know still existed, and the next day, I saw him on a city street.

On the way out, I watch the shadows carefully; I sniff the air and scan the path for tracks.

I do not find any, but that does not mean they are not there; it does not make the Sipsey any less wild, or any less free.

They were probably still hibernating.

6

Burrisizing

THERE CAME A big wind the other day, the kind that sweeps through the woods and makes one tree bend way left while the one next to it bows out to the right. It was a wind without order or direction. A wild wind. I could taste the autumn in it.

It was August 15, a Sunday, around five-thirty in the evening, and I knew as did everyone else that it was hurricane season in Mississippi–all day, hot and pregnant purple thunderclouds had boiled wet and rumbling to the north–but like a petulant child, I insisted on pretending this was not a hurricane-associated wind, but rather, a prelude to autumn.

For some reason, the wind was out of the north.

It had not rained in over three months.

It was going to rain now. A tongue of lightning cracked out of a cloud far to the north. There was no way it couldn't. All around us the sky was like a storm at sea. It was going to rain now; it had to. We had Mother Nature boxed in.

A limb fell to the ground, and broke in half. It was rotten, but still it probably would have dented a car.

"I saw a wind blow a straw through a car windshield in Greenville once," my next door neighbor, Burris, lies. He has come out to join the group of us that is standing by the apartment complex's laundry room, standing outside, waiting and watching. We treat this the way we treat all of his lies, and say nothing. He searches for another lie, for one we will believe.

Why, I do not know. He's always told lies; I've never known him not to lie, given the opportunity. Perhaps he is not impressed with the truth.

Because he is my next door neighbor, and my sidekick, I've taken Burris camping, quite often.

Last summer we went out to the desert of southern Utah. We got sunburned and wind-chafed. We got sand and grit in our hair, in our clothes, in our sleeping bags. At night it was cold. There was a thunderstorm once. Gila monsters were everywhere. For drinking water we had to hike down a gorge to the Dirty Devil River (don't ask how it got its name) and then haul it back up and boil it, and drink it warm. It was nasty; it was awful. Our stomachs cramped. On the trail, hiking, we developed massive gas.

Burris had a great time, though, I know he did, because I had a great time, and he did everything I did. And yet, back home, when people would ask him how the trip went, he'd say awful, and tell them not about the stars in the desert at night or the lunchtime swims in the river, and not about the eerie silence of the twisted rock structures—not about the solitude—but rather, about the bad things.

It was such a good trip he even had to make up the bad things.

"A Gila monster almost bit me," he'd say. This was only a little true. I do not really think the creature was attacking him, I think it was only seeking warmth, but that is not the way Burris tells it. And it was not a Gila monster, it was a horned toad. But to Burris, the Gila monster sounds better.

"Our camp got struck by lightning," he'd say. Again, more Burrisizing. He makes it sound like it knocked our tent down. The lightning bolt hit nearby, yes, about fifty feet away, and if you want to call "camp" everything in a fifty-foot radius, then yes, I suppose lightning did hit our camp, but if you're going to place a boundary on camp, why not call it all of southern Utah? Burris would like that; then he could say lightning was popping and striking all over our campsite. He could say black bears and panthers wandered through camp.

Just because we woke up with frost on our sleeping bags one morning, one morning up high in the shelf country, he told people it snowed. In August.

He said he had a miserable time.

Evidently, Burris believed his audience was like him, and that to impress he had to use something other than the truth. They were impressed, all right, but I believe I could have impressed them just as much by telling them about what really happened.

Perhaps people are impressed by anything, truth and nontruth alike, as long as it is an extreme of some monstrous magnitude. Perhaps Burris can make up and create extremes better than he can observe them.

Or perhaps he does not like people in his desert; he is a crafty codger sometimes. He may have told them all the bad things just to keep them out. He said he had a bad time, yes, an awful time even, but also he did this: he returned with me the next year, to the very same desert.

Burris knows better than to tell his untruths to me. I've got him figured out.

The leaves are coming down in droves, in flocks, like starlings; we can smell the nitrogen-rich smell of thunderstorm, and the gusts turn suddenly cold: there is a front of rain pushing against our wind, not far behind, either, and it super-chills the wind to a delightful temperature. More lightning crackles. Surely this is autumn. People begin to do odd things.

Sarah, a South Jacksonian all her life, a girl who has never even seen the mountains, whoops and runs and jumps fully clothed into the swimming pool, and something crackles in my mind: how did she know to do that? Is it instinctive behavior after all, and not learned, as I was taught? It was like a flashback.

In Logan, Utah, where I went to college, there were lots of mountains and forests and canyons and meadows and rivers and streams. You could see a moose most any time you wanted to. In the fall, out in the marsh, you could count geese at will. How many you want? A dozen? A hundred? A thousand? You got em. Using salmon eggs you could catch cutthroat trout the size of yearling bass, and with rock-rollers and caddis flies, browns too big for a skillet.

There was one river with rapids, the Logan River, that crashed down out of the mountains and into the valley; at the foot of the canyon was a dam, which took and used gratefully the free (more or less) energy of the hard winter's snows high up above treeline. It was a cold river, and a cold lake that backed up against the dam; it was in a national forest, and we'd camp by it a lot on weekends, have parties, good luck pre-exam parties where we'd paint our faces and build a fire and study by firelight and roast marshmallows down by the water's edge. The lake was our totem, of sorts.

I was a member of the Polar Bear Club.

It was not a big club. There were only four of us, but we were like-minded, and that was what mattered: we all felt the same way about the same things. Geese, bull moose in velvet, fly fishing the Logan River, and slim girls who climbed mountains by themselves with their hair braided in pigtails. The first frost of each autumn. The first cold north wind. The first snow.

We'd do it at night. We'd dance around barefooted in the snow, trying to get our courage up, and then, with a good-luck toast for the upcoming year, we'd dive in, all together, on the count of twenty. No clothes were allowed.

It was always a close race to see if we could get back to shore before our muscles locked up, and we became paralyzed. It was bitter cold. Usually, we coughed for weeks.

Ken's a park ranger in Idaho now; Bones, a wildlife technician in Nevada. I haven't heard from Kirby; Alaska I suppose.

Perhaps the girl here at the apartments, Sarah, is, unbeknownst to me, a relative of one of my friends up at the school; perhaps one of them wrote her about how fun it was, and she decided to try it on their advice.

Or maybe it is just something in the wind that made her do it. How I would like to catch it and put it in a bottle, and sniff of it in times of duress. Exams, long grocery lines, traffic on the interstate!

I'd take a whiff each night before bed, too, right before I fell asleep, and then in the morning, upon first awakening.

More people are whooping, hollering, following Sarah's lead, crashing into the pool like lemmings, spilling over the edge one after another after another after another in a variety of dives and near dives: head-first, headlong, backwards, jackknifed, belly flopping. The rain starts to come, it's on us in a flash, but still they are diving in, coming from everywhere—the girl in 3-C, the married couple in 7-G, the policeman in 10-H . . . It's got to be the wind; it's in the air, I tell myself: surely not all of these people have been to north Utah in the fall before.

The rain is a sheet, we're in the middle of a deluge, and lightning cracks dangerously close. The torrent stings the flesh, even through clothes, it's coming down so hard. It's hard to breathe without taking in water. There are only a few of us left seated around the table; most everyone else is in the pool. It's like looking through a windshield in a thunderstorm without the windshield wipers on. Ten yards away I can barely see their heads bobbing up and down in the water, a whole poolful of them: lunatics, all.

Burris defects next. With a shrill, wild whoop, he jumps up from his chair, knocking it over backwards, and goes running toward the pool. He leaps high and wide, far out into the water, and there is a tremendous cheer when he hits. The rain comes down still harder: it is the hardest I've ever seen it rain in my life. It is almost painful, being hit with this much water.

Another tablemate jumps up and sprints for the pool, dives in: I'm left by myself. Trees sway and bend, limbs crack, branches fall: it's cold, as cold as a norther.

A norther. It's August 15, I know, and because I'm more experienced, I know what the people in the pool don't know, that it's not the first cold spell of fall, not really, but the more I think about it, the less I am convinced. Thunder booms. It's my turn. There's cheering, loud cheering, even above the thunder as I shout something about Polar Bears and hit the water in a triple-whammy double-flop.

When I come up for air the water is warm, disgustingly so—Ken and Bones, not to mention Kirby, would be ashamed—but the camaraderie's the same, and it's kind of fun. We laugh at people hurrying by with umbrellas and ask them to come in and join us, reach out for their ankles and try to pull them in.

Ten minutes later the rain has died to a drizzle and the cold wind from the north is gone, swept past. Hattiesburg. Biloxi. Back around to the gulf, full circle. Tomorrow, Argentina. Steam rises from the sidewalks, from the pool itself. The woods drip noisily. The sun comes back out. Suddenly, we feel sheepish.

It was a false alarm. I climb wearily out, as does everyone else, very, very wet, weighted down physically as well as spiritually. I go back to my one-room efficiency apartment, shower, and change. I get a beer from the refrigerator, turn the air conditioner on, flop down on the bed, open my calculus book, and ask myself what in the world am I doing in Jackson, Mississippi, at this time of year.

There is, of course, no answer. I frown and shrug and tell myself it is because Jackson is the best place to do what I do.

Burrisizing.

7

Magic at Ruth Lake

I'M GOING TO tell you about some mountains in northern Utah.

But first, you've got to promise never to visit them. They're my mountains; I adopted them. They are the most majestic mountains in America: the wildest, freest, coldest, oldest, windiest, mountain wildflowerest, mule deerest mountains there are.

Fittingly, they run north-south, the way other North American mountain ranges run. To the north lies a great green sprawl of northern coniferous forests, and beyond that the haze of Wyoming wheatgrass prairie. Beyond that, a few more insignificant rocks, rivers, and mountains such as the Tetons, the Snake and the Yellowstone, and beyond that, Canada.

The closer you get to Canada, the more things'll eat your horse.

I tell you what—I'll do this. I'll tell you how to get to these mountains if you promise not to ever go up there while I'm visiting them. I live in Mississippi, wretched Mississippi (the "M" stands for "Mosquitoes"), and I only get up there three times a year. They are a huge mountain range; with work, there is room for both of us. I drive an orange Volkswagen Rabbit. If you see it parked by the side of the road, keep moving and don't look back. Pretend you never saw it. Natty Bumpo says git.

Except that sometimes I do this: in times of financial liberty, I fly into Salt Lake City (coach fare) and rent a car (subcompact) and drive into the mountains in the little red rent-a-car. Sometimes it is blue, though. Once it was yellow.

I pick the brightly colored little rent-cars because they stand out so well against the violet sky once I get above treeline, once I get up into the tundra and alpine meadows above 12,500 feet.

So I will do this: so that you will know it is my car, so that you can steer plenty clear of me, I'll put a pretty fair-sized rock on the hood of the car. A rock that you cannot help but see. It will be like an old Indian signal, like a trail sign: Do Not Enter.

I'll put an old rag under the rock so it doesn't scratch the paint.

Now I'll tell you about my adopted mountains. They cover many thousands of square miles, and have places in them with names like this: Moon Lake, Laughing Coyote Uplift. Wolf Tooth Creek, Spirit Lake, and the Lost Elk Caves. Lake of the Gods, and the Screaming River. Blue Hole. Lolo Pass.

Lolo Pass is, I suppose, as good a place as any to fall in love with someone.

Thunderstorms are spectacular and beautiful up in the jagged rocky peaks. They get about two per year.

They are the oldest mountains our country has; if we—and I'm considering getting a bill started in Congress—ever decided to have a National Mountain Range, this would have to be them. They're Precambrian, before Life; they've almost always been here.

Also, there's lots of bald eagles. Hiking down a narrow rushing stream, sometimes you spook them up out of dead trees. They fly off with great strong wingbeats. It is really something you should see, the way they fly.

There are a lot of dead trees up high in this mountain range. Big, dead trees, as if size and strength and age are no insurance against the winters.

I am presently trying to learn to use understatement in my writings. I believe this is a good point to practice.

Winters are harsh.

The only way into these mountains is through one of two roads. One gravelly frost-heaved road gingerly and innocently skates its way up through the western quarter of the range, going (most of the time) north-south. The other one delicately skirts the northern boundaries.

It, too, is a two-laner. It's a bad place to have a busted water hose, a bad place to have a flat. There are no gas stations, there are no cafés. There is nothing that is not beautiful.

I've been up there and been snowed on in July, and August. Snowed on hard.

The two little skeins of roads that lead into the area usually close up in early November, but sometimes late October. The area sleeps un-disturbed, protected under a sheet of snow and ice for as many as seven to eight months each year. It seems to me that all this ice and snow and beauty sleep preserves it, and resculpts it a little, and makes it a little more awesome each spring.

Except that spring sometimes does not come until the Fourth of July.

And yes, it does have glaciers.

It is mind-boggling to pick up a slab of rock and find in it an ancient brachiopod, a fossil of one of the earliest, most primitive sea creatures ever known, and realize that these mountains in the heartland of the United States of America were once a coastline.

Sometimes, it really makes me quite dizzy.

There's got to be a strange and long-lost history about the place; sometimes, working my way through a narrow niche in a sheer cliff wall between two wild and empty valleys, threading my way down a talus slope as a snow-dusting August storm comes rolling in low and foggy, rolling in to meet me, then sometimes I will begin crying for no reason. A terrible sadness wrenches from me, and I have to get away from the place and down to one of the meadows below me before the feeling is gone.

Other times, I start to laugh almost uncontrollably. I lean back against a tree in one of the forests and feel the rough hard texture of the bark pressing against my back and the warm forest pine straw beneath me, and for many minutes the woods will roar with great hearty booming laughs: my laughs. Laughs the likes of which Jackson, Mississippi, has never heard.

They are magic mountains.

You would not believe the alpenglow in the evenings.

The sunrises are pretty neat, too.

Once, while hiking down a dark and narrow corridor of a game trail, with dense tall sweet-smelling Doug firs and blue spruce on either side, and little blue mountain primroses for a carpet beneath me, I looked up to see someone standing in the trail ahead of me. In the shadows. It was just a silhouette.

Only it wasn't a someone; it was a doe mule deer. I stopped, and then walked closer. She did not run.

I got to within thirty or forty yards of her before she turned and ran down the trail.

I do believe it was the first time she had ever seen a human.

There are lots of good things about these mountains, but the best are the lakes.

There are lots of lakes.

Little lost slipper-sized things, they are cold and blue and clear and have lily pads around the shore and lots of fish in them.

The fish are quite tasty. The water is delicious. In November, when snow clouds come rolling in in the mornings, you can sit down on the shoreline, crouched behind a boulder or a tree, and see ducks, mallards mostly, come whistling in to splash down on the lakes.

From September to April there is ice on the ponds. Halloween weekends are the best: they are almost always frozen over by then, with a good smooth soft white blanket of snow to boot, and it is fun to go tramp words out in the middle of one of the little lens-shaped lakes. There is just one after the other after the other—they lie in chains, one- to ten-acre depressions in the glacial slickrock, usually at the base of steep cirques and cliffs.

I once spent two weeks in the summer traveling from lake to lake, fishing with spoons and spinners. I came out of the woods on the east end of the range sunburned, bearded, and twenty pounds heavier, and still I had not resolved which way I liked Utah trout best: broiled on a hot flat rock, or deep fried in bacon grease for breakfast. Toward the end of the trip I ran out of bacon grease; it was a shame, too, because I had almost been ready to make my decision.

It is clear to me that my only option is to go back and try it again. Start from scratch. I will bring more bacon grease this time.

I mentioned that these are magic mountains. They are. The rocks are magic, the lakes are magic, the wind and snow and trees are magic . . . they will all talk to you, if you listen right.

A farm boy from Indiana, of all places, taught me to listen. He was a friend of Ken's and mine, my first year up at school, up at Utah State. I had applied to U.S.U. because it was the campus closest to the mountains I had seen in the movie *Jeremiah Johnson*.

He had applied to U.S.U. because once he had gone fishing for an afternoon in one of the little mountain lakes while driving crosscountry through the area with his cousin. Surely you will agree with me that it takes a great deal of magic to do that, to make a farmboy from Indiana and a city boy from Texas apply to a school two thousand miles away from home just because of a one-day fishing trip and a two-hour movie, respectively.

Once they get into you, they are as jealous as a lover; they will never let you look at other mountains again, and you will never want to.

When you are away from them, they will be all you think about. Weeks, months, even years will be measured in terms of how long you've been away, and how long it is till you return.

Now you see why I am hesitant to give you their name. Their beauty is a curse as well as a blessing. No one ever forgets them.

The farm boy's name was Rob. Rob Samuelson. His family was from Sweden, and he said *ja* instead of yeah. He had played basketball for the state high school 4-A champions in Indiana and could carry a seventy-five-pound backpack up a steep trail all day long and then sing songs around the campfire until dawn. He played the guitar. His favorite food was Dinty Moore beef stew. He would actually giggle whenever he smelled it cooking, simmering in the campfire, with fir branches snapping and aspen logs popping at night.

Also, I forgot to tell you this about these mountains: at night, there are more stars over them than anywhere else in the world, it is a fact. A tall man can jump up and almost reach them. Rob used to try, quite often.

"Too much Dinty Moore," I would tell him when he missed. He weighed 245 pounds.

We were freshmen, and had been in Utah three days when we made our first trip into the, into these, mountains. We drove up maple-studded Logan Canyon, wound around royal blue Bear Lake, breezed down into the dusky sage country of southwestern Wyoming, and suddenly, there we were, at the north entrance.

They sprawled across the southern horizon like a jagged chain of bluish snow-tipped biceps. Big Biceps.

We stopped the car and got out and looked at them. We were still fifty miles off, and they looked huge. It was cold and still out; it was evening, and there was chill in the air. There was no traffic. We watched them, stunned, as if waiting for them to do something— move toward us to greet us? break into song and dance? take a bow?— but when they did not, we got cold and got back in the car and hurried on.

Once we reached the forested regions and started up the switchbacks, we zipped up our down jackets to stay warm and rolled the windows down so we could smell the trees.

Surely our mere graduating from high school did not merit this reward; there had to be some catch. We were incredulous. A herd of mule deer, all does, ran across the road in front of us, panicked, darted back off the road, and ran along the woodline beside us for a while, wild-eyed, before slipping back into the woods.

It was the first time in my life I had ever seen mule deer; I could not believe my good fortune. It was like a graduation present, like a much-thought-over birthday gift. I was eighteen.

No one should live to be eighteen without seeing these mountains. It should be a national law.

We drove past little turnouts for trucks and sightseers; we groaned up peaks and idled down passes. There were no side roads, no logging roads: just wild country, and mountains, and lakes.

Grandaddy Lake. Mirror Lake. Lost Pine Lake.

Ruth Lake. ¾ Mile.

We stopped at the Ruth Lake trail. It was getting late. There was a place by the wooden trail sign that was big enough for two or three cars to pull off onto; there was a ridge. The cliffs behind us, on the other side of the road, were beginning to glow. It frightened me; I thought something was wrong with them.

I had never seen alpenglow before.

We chocked the car tires with rocks and slipped our packs on and hurried up the trail like prisoners let out of jail. We did not look back.

When you visit these mountains, bring a down coat or parka, and gloves, and heavy socks and a ski cap, no matter what time of year it is.

The ground felt hard and frozen under our boots; our breath came in shallow bursts of exhaled cloud vapor, and our nostril hairs froze together when we inhaled. It was turning colder; the sun was going down. The air tasted delicious. I felt quite dizzy; quite giddy. I felt like I never wanted to leave these mountains.

Ahead of me, Rob hurried along the trail. He was in a hurry to get to Ruth Lake. He had not eaten since lunch. He had a whole case of Dinty Moore beef stew in his pack.

I'm not even going to tell you how beautiful Ruth Lake was, you wouldn't believe it. We came around a corner and suddenly there it was, in the middle of the forest. A cow elk and calf on the other end of the lake looked up in alarm and whirled and galloped off across a little meadow before disappearing into the trees. Long after they were gone we could still hear timber crashing and hooves striking rock.

It was not a big lake, but standing beside it, we felt tiny. We were awed by its beauty, not its size. A cold wind was gusting across the water, dancing toward us; it made our noses tingle and our cheeks flush. Rob took his pack off and began scouting for firewood. There was plenty to be found. There are lots of live trees in these mountains, but there are a lot of dead ones too.

It is a very old place. The Precambrian outcroppings are at least two billion years old. We sat down in a grove of trees by the lake's edge and listened to and smelled the stew simmering, and listened to the breezes, and watched the lake, and for a little while, the stars. It was very cold. Coals would pop and crackle, and sparks would float up into the night. The stew was good. After we had finished it we watched the fire and talked about what we were going to study. When we went to bed, the stars were gone; there were grey slippers of clouds tumbling down out of the taller mountains like frost-fog boiling out of an open freezer. When we woke up in the morning, it was snowing. I went bonkers. I had never seen snow before.

Rob was playing basketball that year, and I football; we had to be back by noon. He packed while I ran around in the snow and threw snowballs and slid in it and ate it and kicked it like sand. Then we hiked out. There was fog everywhere; it was still snowing.

There were lots of animal tracks out. I took care not to step in them. The tallest of the late-season meadow flowers poked up through the snow. I guessed there to be a foot of snow on the ground. Rob said it was an inch and a half. I fell down several times.

It was sunny and dry back down in the valley, back on campus; no snow had fallen. No one believed us when we told them it had snowed up in the mountains.

Of course, if anyone had asked us how to get to Ruth Lake, we would have given them the wrong directions.

We were already making plans for next week.

I've been all over northern Utah since then, all over these mountains in all types of seasons and weather: the Upper Fork of the Weber River, discovered by trapper Pete Skene Ogden, that lucky devil, and other places too.

Jim Bridger used to live in these mountains, over on the eastern flanks, near where Fort Bridger used to be. And there's King's Peak, the highest point in Utah; 13,528 feet. I've been to all of these places in my adopted mountains, over and over. There's still one thing I always do once each year, though; I always make one special overnight trip to Ruth Lake, and I always pitch my tent down in the trees by the water's edge and build a fire in the same place and watch the lake by moonlight and listen to the wind. I always bring a can of Dinty Moore beef stew and, silently, I toast Rob with a Sierra Club cup full of crystal-cold lake water.

It is still always my best trip of the year.

8

The Grizzly Cowboys

I

I GOT THIS letter, from the Forest Service. They said they would send me out with some of their people, in a forest where grizzlies used to be, and sheep now are, if I'd write about it, and draw the picture.

So in July this girl from Mississippi and I are out on horses and this big old silver-bearded mountain man named Jenkins is pulling a pack-string of government mules with one forearm while the other tugs the reins of his black horse, Dime, who is twenty years old and muscled, very large, and spirited, too much so. Mountain air. Jenkins (Wayne) himself is sixty-one. He calls the mules wicked names when they are bad.

A camera hangs around Elizabeth's neck. There is a notepad in my pocket. The Forest Service wants me to tell people what bears are like, sheep too. I know my assignment, and frown, and concentrate on it, but it's the people I keep seeing, even out here.

There are, in this one wilderness area, almost two million acres and hundreds of black bears, but only six (maybe) grizzly bears. On the horses, there's Elizabeth and me, and Wayne, and Gary and Bob. They've got us outnumbered by one. It would be nice to say we are all on the same side, but that's not entirely correct. We would like to be, but the bear doesn't want us, won't take us. Like the wisest of our dreams, surely the grizzly realizes that to depend on us would doom him; to depend on anything, even a lucky break in the winter, would doom a grizzly, and make him a thing less than he fully is.

These woods are different, riding through a field, buck-and-rail fence behind us, just before we enter the trees; the last bit of mountains we see are the Tetons—and the horses step over fallen trees, downed and rotting timber. There are slow streams, backed up from the workings of beaver, and we splash through these, and we shift and creak in our saddles, that good noise, and the woods are different because there are bears in them. Grizzlies. I don't, didn't, know that six of anything could make as much of a difference as can six grizzly bears, even spread through an entire state, a whole country.

It's good policy, to keep around a thing that knows how to keep from dooming itself. When birds called, or fluttered in the brush, we were conscious of the noise, the sound. All sounds were important. We listened to everything. I knew the big mountains were above me, ahead and high through the trees, and I could feel the different air masses, sliding down off of them, at different times in the day. I could feel everything. I felt like an Indian, and was glad and grateful for everything, and cannot explain why.

If one of those six bears was a female, and had cubs, we could have eight bears in these woods, this forest, if both cubs lived, and survived.

Everything happened too fast. It is now one year since that trip and I am writing this, as Barry Hannah says, only as an obligation to the people who put the trip together, and who are waiting to see what I have to say, something that has never been said before. Which can't be done. "It's the crown jewel of American wildlife, fierce, noble, instills fear, respect," etc., *magnificent:* you can lay the words out as if on a Scrabble board, or put them in a bag and shake them up. Be sure and include *majestic*.

Instead I will write about the people I was with, who are trying to save the bear, those six bears. They're not a mirror of the grizzly, but close. You can sit around with them and watch them whittle or talk about camp cooking or shoeing a horse and then, sometimes, you can almost see the bear, if he is indeed still out there. The way the moon would sometimes come up over the mountains: I *thought* I could kind of picture what one would look like, in the wild. I have to confess that it was a feeling, as seemingly transparent as it was, that nonetheless you could hold on to. Miraculous. Sleeping in those woods was new. Do we have much left that is new? You can't forever do away with your old, either. What I am saying is that I just wish we would move a little more carefully, with our grizzly bears.

As beautiful as the mountains were, and as real as the saddles creaking and dust rising seemed and felt—it was still the nights that were the smoothest, clearest, and purest. In the tent, I would lie awake, after Jenkins and Foli and Bob had cooked for us, and cleaned up, and were preparing the horses for the night, feeding them a little oats—and I would look up at my tent ceiling and know pretty well that there could be a grizzly nearby—they saw one, not twenty miles from the very creek we're above, last summer! Never mind the creek's name—and if you think we, humans, didn't come out of those woods too, in our past, then you're disowning something. There was steak caught in my teeth one night and I broke off a twig and picked it free.

There were stars and muted campfire noises down by the horses and I was often at night up on little hill and over in the next valley I suppose sheepherders were watching the sheep and I was reaching back to my past, because it had to be pretty much as it was a hundred years ago, and it wasn't sliced away from the rest of us yet. I was *doing* it. There was bacon and egg and fried potatoes in my stomach, and the taste of them still there.

You could write your congressmen, and western congressmen. You could probably find their addresses, and sit down and write. You could rent a helicopter, too. You could fly over the wilderness before first snow, even in late summer, sprinkling dead sheep, far into the wilderness, sailing them down, spiraling, into the treetops below. There is the theoretical and then there is the pragmatic. One tastes better and is more comfortable and the other keeps you alive. It's no secret which of the two the grizzlies would prefer. •

The horses were beautiful, even for horses. They would put these things on them, as dusk fell and fireflies began to dance, called Mormon hobbles, magician-style handcuffs that were quite simple to snap loose, if you knew the trick – neither the horses nor the Indians ever figured the trick out, only the Mormons – the harder you pulled, the tighter they got, but when you pushed against them (on them) in a certain and light way, they literally fell off, mystically, and the horses stepped free – and in the evenings the horses, when first hobbled, would take off in great prancing leaps, front and back legs bound together, so that it looked like a new species of animal, unicorns, perhaps, the green meadows in which they were hobbled were that beautiful, and their odd lunges, and the clanking sounds, leaping, gathering, leaping, gathering, trying to outleap the hobbles . . . Wayne and Gary and Bob sitting around, tired, watching them, holding their coffee cups, just watching them . . . after a while the horses would quiet down, and gather, and commiserate, and begin grazing . . .

Elizabeth and I could smell those stars and cold air currents rolling down off the mountains. I wanted more of it, all I could get.

In the morning there was sun. Those bastards back at work were probably milling around with their noses in each other's behinds, like dogs. Sons of rotting bitches! It was good to be tightening a horse's cinch strap, in the morning. It was great. I pulled it real tight; slapped him in the belly, to make him suck up harder, and pulled quickly tighter, again.

It was Gary's (Foli's) turn to make breakfast. It was the second day. We were to ride very deep into the wilderness: days and days. Jenkins and Bob were older, and were easing into the trip. You could tell it took them two days and a certain amount of miles to relax. Leaving something behind: going back to another thing. Having the opportunity, the availability, option, to do so.

Jenkins lights a pipe. There aren't any bears in this story. He begins to sing, and has not even been drinking.

You know the way dust rises on a trail, from a horse's hooves. One of the mules, the chief and balky one, was named "Hooger." To hear Jenkins get mad and bellow: Hooger! Go out in the woods sometime and pretend the mule is being a real ass, say he has bitten you, or emptied your pots all over the mountain because a butterfly has startled him, or pretend he is merely wreaking havoc on the other mules, biting and kicking them for pleasure. Pretend black blinding anger, and cut loose: yell that Hooger word. It will scare the bears off, but it sounds good, coming up out of your chest and out your throat. This is sort of what the woods were like, with Wayne, and Bob, and Gary.

Bob was from Vietnam—not born there—born in Idaho, his brother guides a raft on fishing trips down a river. Bob used to be a cowboy, the kind that holds on to bulls—and he's the range expert. He looks at plants and knows their name, and how much water they require, can tell you what's been eating them and if there's a dearth or abundance of it.

You can't look at Bob and not know that he wasn't in Vietnam. Somehow, it is a part of him, and in his gaze, even when he does something simple, like watches the fire, or cleans dishes, or puts his foot in the stirrup of a saddle. But, he is very happy. You can tell this too, by these same things, same sights. He deserves this. The word is dues. I am sure that he thought about this Idaho place, often, over there. It probably doesn't even matter if the old bear survives or not. I know that is not what they wanted me to say and it is not what I believe or wish in my heart and I didn't even have any intention of saying it myself but now I am thinking of Bob, over there, thinking about these mountains, and rivers, and the way fires smell, and cold mornings, and though yes, the woods are better for him because he knows there is grizzly in them, the other part ain't too bad, and could have maybe brought him around on his own. Maybe. Probably. Not as quickly, for sure, but probably, and just as far. Maybe. I think.

People who have been through tough times but are finally at peace sure do have that look about them.

II

There's a man named Emry Davis up in these mountains. That is how his name is spelled. He wears red suspenders and is short and chesty and chews. His dogs, being sheepdogs, each have one yellow eye and one blue eye. He is his father's father's grandson, and is sixty. They've always herded sheep in these mountains, since the 1800s. There are blue lakes up above tree line, with scattered moraine, and flowers.

The grass in the meadows is like a carpet. You want to roll in it, on your back, and there are hawks above you. It is a good country. Emry Davis runs three thousand sheep through this wilderness early in the summer. His family used to run thirty thousand, then ten thousand. The three thousand still sounds like a lot. It's a pretty big piece of country, though.

If Emry Davis kills a grizzly he goes to jail along with everyone in his outfit: nephews, sons. They aren't the sort of men who would like that kind of action. The movie *Tom Horn*. Gary and Bob and Wayne ride herd on the sheepherders. The thing is working. The sheep thing. Everything clicks. If only there were bears to thunder across the tall grass, down through the creeks. Chasing elk. Ripping at logs, roaring. Being bears.

Emry rides through the aspen, the breezes, doing his job up here. The sheep do gain, on these rich cool high meadows. He's never seen a grizzly up here. His father used to see them often, and had stories.

They, the sheep, never stay in one place for more than a night. Bob doesn't let them take the range down. Gary rides through the night, with field glasses, watches the herders, the sheep, ranges back and ahead, looking for sign, tracks, fur, kills. He calls if he finds even the suspicion of grizzly and everybody—sheep, rangers, FBI agents lurking in the woods (seriously: Emry displays some of the business cards they tack to trees in his camp, during the day, while he is out herding—to let him know he is being watched—Hello, Crockett, Tubbs? This is Castillo. We've got a problem)—Emry shakes, as he shows the cards, creased and old and accumulated, in his wallet—he is only a man who lives in the woods and fields and raises his sheep in the wilderness—if a bear is sighted, or sign thereof—grizzly, not black—all of these people, players in the mountains, get the hell out of the woods. Make way for the bear.

I think Wayne is there because he is older, gruff, knows all about horses, the woods, and life. He doesn't know the Latin names of the plants as does Bob and can't fix the communications equipment like Gary can, but Wayne directs things nonetheless.

The man who understands horses is in charge of the mission.

The plot and counterplot is sinfully human and complex to take place back in the good old mountains. Gary is trying to undo the damage an ambitious grad student, who was the bear monitor before him, has done, with what are now obviously false reportings of grizzly sign. Gary spends five to ten times the amount of hours in the woods that the previous monitor did, and lives day and night looking, not just eight-hour days as was the previous monitor's schedule, in the forest; and in three years he has seen grizzly tracks once. The grad student who reported the plethora of grizzly fur, scratchings, scat, etc., has a very comfortable job now. It looked damn good on his resume.

Oh well. The bears can take this, must, along with all the other bullshit. They have been shot at, poached, lied to, tranquilized, dropped from helicopters during transplanting (a process whereby the federal government tells an eight-hundred-pound animal used to feeding on thousand-pound elk and mountainsides of green vegetation where it needs to go, and to stay put). Jenkins has seen a wild bear up here once in seventeen years—coincidentally, seventeen years ago, his first year on this job—and she was on a streamside, a long way off, in the morning sun—his hands move as he describes it, and it was almost a religious experience, you sense—flipping over boulders with one paw, boulders that three or four strong men wouldn't ever be able to budge, and the little cubs (two) would then rush in and pounce on mice, chase crickets and beetles, whatever was beneath the boulders. Wayne and his father, who was eighty then, watched the mother move all the way down the streamside and into the woods; the meadow looked afterward as if it had been mined: boulders strewn, some having tumbled all the way down into the stream. The sun on her long claws. Wayne said he was a hundred yards away, up in the trees, on a ledge, and was terrified. His father said he used to see them pretty often like that, as a young man.

Can you define the bear, in his absence, by the people, and country, around him? Probably not. But for me, they are the only clues. The little clickety 16 mm films in the Forest Service headquarters: I watched them for eight hours, one Sunday—they take your breath away, but after a while, all the muscle, all the carnage—the two bears fighting over a dead elk they have found, racing back and forth across the stream with it in their jaws, dragging its half ton like a dog pulling his bedding around—becomes hypnotic. It isn't until you step back out of the building and look up at the mountains that you can ever consider what the bear is like.

On the second day, Elizabeth is walking oddly: when we mount up, she winces, and rides bravely for two minutes before giving up and pulling her down sleeping bag out of the pack and piling it up around her saddle.

"We'll rub a little whiskey on your behind tonight, and it'll be fine," Wayne assures her, seriously. She looks at me, then at Wayne, but Wayne is looking straight ahead, then back at the mules, tugging, urging Hooger on.

"He is probably kidding," I tell her, later. These mountains. We had pancakes for breakfast.

"What do you do for a living anyway, Rick?" Gary asks sleepily. Lunch: peanut butter sandwiches. Warm water. My eyelid flickers: my left hand jumps. For some reason I'm unable to answer him. Elizabeth watches me cautiously: hands me a piece of her candy bar. Finally, instead, I just tell him this:

"At work, they make up stories about each other, and tell them to the bosses, trying to get each other in trouble, trying to get ahead by putting someone else down. They hardly ever do anything *productive*. They just make up these horrible stories, and rumors."

Wayne shakes his head and looks disgusted. Bob looks off at the woods. Gary is incredulous. The woods feel suddenly different: I should not have mentioned it, put it into words. A horse stamps, nickers, paws: dust rises.

We are about thirty miles into the woods before they are able to begin talking about the office part of their own lives. I think about my office life, and ride, and listen. They have named some of the mules in the string for people in their office. Fortunately Hooger is not one of them. And we can't even flip boulders over: but expect the bear to coexist, to fit where we tell it to fit? To not go along a certain stream? We can roast sheep over a fire out here at night, ten thousand feet up, but expect the grizzly to not even wander across any of the three thousand that have come into his high green country this summer?

Surprisingly—or perhaps not—he does not. The thick presence of all the black bears is as condemning a sign as any: radio-collar studies have shown that black bears, when a grizzly moves into their area, fall over themselves getting out of the territory. They don't even wait for daylight. They flee. One collared black bear made fifty miles before dawn.

I like to think that if from anywhere on their range the grizzlies can see a road, a town, smoke rising, they leave: the true wild bears, the ones that have not been tampered with, experimented upon.

Some people say the various "bear teams" have committed two major mistakes—the first understandable, the second unforgivable—done sheerly out of politics and meanness, knowing full well the consequences—it surprises me that none of the slain campers' families ever filed suit, for manslaughter, or worse—have been one, trying to transplant drugged, tranquilized bears to places less distant than the moon or its equivalent, and two—simply not wanting to back down from a memo—closing the dumps at Yellowstone. It doesn't even need discussing. The Craighead brothers—John and Frank, for a long time the foremost and only grizzly experts in the country—told the Park Service to close the eyesore dumps slowly, and for office reasons, the Park Service didn't, and instead shut them down entirely, overnight, taking them away—and the fat and healthy and numerous bears spilled, like prizes from a cereal box, hungry and aggressive and sassy and portly, accustomed to being around people, into the general lowland countryside. Hello, pilgrims.

This occurring about the time Bob was going over the big pond in a bomber, wearing camouflage. It shocked the bears' system, and if they are to recover from it, the dumps, so runs the argument, will need to be re-established—not the hideous park refuse centers, but their nutritive equivalents, back deep in the wild high alone places, where the bear belongs, where he deserves to be, where he came from. So that he can help define what is still high and alone. The dumps lured nearly all the grizzlies out of the mountains; the Park Service took the dumps away, and killed the bears; there aren't many left—not enough females left in Yellowstone to field a healthy football team . . .

Sheep carcasses, cattle, road-killed elk and deer; the great winterkills of the Madison River elk—by dropping these things a hundred miles into the woods, the bears might meet each other, reproduce, feed, and survive, and grow back into the system from which they came in the first place, a system that *could* hold them, but doesn't, because they're down, reproductively speaking, to zero. (About twenty-five breedable females in the Yellowstone ecosystem—forty-three cubs.) This idea might not work, and should be filed away somewhere for the horrible, possible future—no one is in favor of it, at present—but it should be filed, should be heard, and considered. If the bears don't come out of it themselves, it could be the next thing to try.

Even Emry Davis, the pragmatic old sheepherder, admits that it is a way to save them, the bears, what one might at first suppose is his enemy. Every bear that is shot by black bear hunters, every bear that is killed by humans, seems to be a female, as their exposure is so much greater than that of the males: gathering more food, for the demands of reproduction, of saving the species.

There is frustration on Wayne's (and Bob's and Gary's) part. They want to see action, effort, not debate. Too many stuffed shirts: too many people afraid of making a mistake, creating controversy, and losing their "jobs," as did the Craigheads (what a lovely name). I think of my office. No purity left: not where it counts. Or not where it's effective. Gary, riding out on his horse: searching for fur. A hundred and fifty miles from a pay phone.

"The biggest problem is that the line of control is not narrow enough," says Wayne. It is a growl. There's sun: we're on a ridge, looking out over the western United States. We saw a cigarette pack by an old campfire a while back. We're not deep enough yet. Not for me, not for them, and certainly, then, not for the bear.

"A few years ago there were too damn many bosses, always working against each other, following different plans. Now there's another group—the Interagency Grizzly Bear Committee—since 1983—which is trying to work together with everyone—coordination—the Fish and Wildlife people, the Forest Service, the Park Service, the BLM . . . "

There's still squabbling. But it will get better. It has to.

Wayne is getting windy. He's been thinking about it for years, and sees it like a vision. "You always do best when one man—just one, a good one – is in charge of it. That one man might make a mistake here and there, but it's the staticness, and neutrality of the situation, that can be fatal."

The bear is perfectly capable of just fading away; it's a thing we know, and fear.

We ride. Hawks soar on warm currents. We are in short sleeves. Elizabeth's camera snicks: taking pictures of ripped-up logs, scratches on trees – black bears, black bears, tame and wan. It seems that along the trail every third tree is scratched by bears: deep scratches, that make you stare. One set extends above our heads, even seated on the horses. The smell of black bear does not alarm the horses, the mules. How they know to fear the grizzly, an animal they have never seen, I do not understand, but would like to learn. Bears freeze to death in the winter, from the hard conditions, and nutrition is so critical that even one good three-day meal – an elk, a deer, a couple of sheep – can make the difference, and carry them through, roll them across the winter of sleep, and into the spring, one more year of many.

III

Sheep love to die, it seems to me. I'm listening to John Burns. This man is the boss. We're in St. Anthony, before the trip. There seems to be an itching almost-anger, practiced resignation, that he cannot go, that he cannot be in two places at once, and do more. He has met me at six A.M. to talk about the problem, and the forest, and he deploys men and women, cuts trees as he thinks they, the cuttings, will best aid the grizzlies (six), rather than the Forest Service – this in the times of cutting back. There are computers in every office, but John Burns deploys the people. It's a nice small Idaho town.

John Burns is talking about sheep, about the ways they can die. He begins to tick them off on his fingers, but gives that up. "They run up to coyotes, wanting to play. They fall over in stream crossings and forget to get back up, and drown. They die giving birth. They die of fright, of thunder. The sight of lightning kills some. They blunder into large black bears. Their most famous and practiced trick is suffocation: they get bottlenecked somewhere, a place too narrow for them to all fit, but they keep pouring in anyway, *trying* to fit: they climb up on top of each other's backs, and crush those below, and suffocate them. You can lose two-thirds of your herd inside five minutes, that way." And I think: they worship death.

The grizzly has killed people before, the grizzly has killed sheep. It takes an expert to keep a herd alive in the mountains, and sometimes bears get blamed for losses they didn't cause. But they will kill sheep. They like to eat them.

John Burns has an ashtray made from the plaster cast of a grizzly track taken several years ago. It is the size of a tennis racquet. His forest totals 1,837,000 acres. The six or less bears are his number-one priority. An American hero. It is possible that all six are males. I think, leaving his office, that I wish he had at least a hundred to work with: to start over, and correct mistakes. There were seven, but some-one shot and wounded a radio-collared mother, who died in her den over the winter from malnutrition. Which was fortunate, because her cubs consumed her, in the den, and didn't die from same. But what will they do next year? There have been several sightings of these cubs around a certain lake, which is heavy black bear hunt-ing country. Over in Yellowstone, the count is twenty-five sows and forty-three cubs. We've got to hold tight, do the right thing, there. The forty-three cubs is a good number; but the twenty-five sows—that worries me. And that's the *highest* sighting in years—an improvement.

More. I want more. More chaos, more anarchy.

More honor, more strength. We can get it right. We can go into the woods without being mauled, without ruining things. I want the bear to give us one more chance.

Can you doom a grizzly, by touching him: by allowing him to have nonfatal interaction (tranquilization, capture) with humans, and be released? It appears no amount of cannons and fireworks, rifle shots, even pain, can deter a grizzly after surviving a human handling: does he remember the fact that he escaped, and was therefore stronger? And is no longer afraid? Certainly, he's not afraid. You have to admire their straight-ahead belief in themselves. It has gotten them further than we have gone, yet. Almost all of the "problem bears" have been created by human touch—garbage in camps, in towns—at one time or another. It is time to stop handling bears. The Interagency Grizzly Bear Committee, for example, is trying to limit the number of radio-collared grizzlies in the wild to ten.

If you see a little bear, a cub, in the woods, and you've got a tree, you could go up it: because the mother will never be far away, and she'll be very, very angry, if and when she discovers you nearby. Or, because grizzlies (and blacks) can climb, you could instead lie down, and try to present as harmless a presence as possible. The bear can hit thirty miles an hour; running is never an option.

Maybe if she sees you, and you lie down, or stand very still, she'll leave. Or she might charge, bluffing. Or she might charge, not backing off, and then do some chewing, some swatting. Be very quiet, and cover your vital organs by crouching: one hand over the back of your neck. Some people make it out this way, some don't. A game warden up in Glacier killed a radio-collared male at point blank with six shots from a .357 magnum. It was the sixth shot he got lucky on, snapping the neck. Big gun. (He was letting the bear out of a cage).

So I don't think much of weapons, with regard to grizzlies. I say, let him chew. Because if you start firing away and don't get lucky with that fifth shot, or sixth, then he'll eat you for sure, all of you, and then deposit you in his scat, all over the West.

If you lie still, and don't fight, he might take only a rib; a piece of shoulder. I had a professor once who got up on a meadow with the wind all wrong, and cubs in the area, and he was mauled. A research graduate student was with him, down below the meadow, and he saved the professor's life by sneaking up behind some bushes and roaring–like another bear–and frightening her away. The professor said it was a sound like the cracking of an egg–the bear's jaws, popping his skull: and the heat, and the breath.

They got the professor out by helicopter. A lot of people–most of them–do live through a grizzly attack. The professor lived, and teaches. He acknowledges, gratefully, that it was his fault. And he doesn't go out in the meadows, up high like that, with a strong breeze behind him, anymore.

In fact, he says, all strong breezes like that one rattle him.

Don't take a dog with you into bear country. The dog runs around, sniffs up a bear, surprises it, is frightened, and runs back to you. With a surprise hot on his tail. Look what I have brought you, Dad. And human menstrual periods seem to provoke investigation, as do sexual odors.

We are dealing with an animal that came from Europe and Asia in the Ice Age, over the Bering Strait, like the rest of us, and into the tundra and glaciers: as wide and open a country as has ever existed, a world of ice. Increased size and aggression were the only ways to defend one's self, to develop with such a country: nowhere to hide. Every cell of a grizzly remembers his past, those times, and we will have to be very patient, letting him develop again, in response to yet another new environment: furtiveness, and avoidance. Both sides are trying hard, with transgressions of course in either camp: it is just that the bear's camp is so much smaller. The larger grizzlies are being selected against; the plots of their average weight are declining, plummeting, down over ten pounds a year. They are getting there. They *are* becoming smaller, less aggressive, more furtive: it is just a quickly downhill race to see if they run out of individuals before they get there.

Veins race across the horses' legs and chests, standing in sun. "Everyone is so nice," says Elizabeth. It is the day before we leave.

There are spurs, on the grizzly cowboys out here, Wayne and Bob and Gary. The mules and horses have *U.S.* branded on their flanks. In the winter, Wayne travels to Tennessee, to shop for stock. We sit in the shade; the horses stand in the sun, and fidget. It is another century.

Off in the woods, the sandhill cranes begin to howl and flap; birds of tremendous size, happy in a country of great size. There is a breeze. Bob and Wayne talk awhile. We are closer to the valley again, looping around, heading back. In two days we will be in a car, driving, on a road. Wayne is talking about retirement: figuring out the logistics. Please no.

"Oh, I'm so big, so old, so tired," Wayne groans, that night. "Used to be I'd dance eight of ten dances." He has told his wife that when he gets back, he will take her dancing. "Now I'm only good for two out of ten." He shakes his head mournfully, but then, brightening, asks us if we have heard the story about the man who used to have this job of his, of being a grizzly cowboy, before he did.

"No," we tell him.

Wayne chuckles. "He was a tough old booger: he would definitely dance ten out of ten. First and only time we ever met him, we were camped up above Boone Crick with the herders, about sundown, and this guy comes racing down through the woods and downed timber riding a sow grizz, whipping her with a rattlesnake, and he grabs a cup and scoops up a gulp of sheep dip, downs it, tosses the cup away and takes off again, saying, 'Sorry to eat and run, boys, but I've got to go, there's a mean sucker after me.'"

IV

One thing is for certain: after the second day, you do not ever want to come out. Bob tells me about whortleberry plants: points them out. If I were a bear, I would eat them. They look delicious. Summer.

"How's the load?" Wayne, leading the string, calls back. He means are any of the tents or packs slipping off. Hooger is bad about crow-hopping: turning sideways and bucking, in a tight little prance, until all the pans spill. Coffee and beans, and tin cans and pots. Perhaps he likes the noise.

"Fine," comes the answer, Bob, immediately, comfortably. Bob in the back, watching, instinctively, also judging the range. A team. Gary off alone, casting, youngest, much energy: riding across and back, up and ahead, back, looking. The horses and mules break into trots at seemingly regular intervals. The woods are right this morning. There are yellow flowers. Gary points out claw marks on a tree.

The last day. Hooger misbehaving, trying to run all the way. A cabin up ahead: riding through deep green grass, crossing beaver streams. The mountains tall and white behind us. I twist, turn in my saddle, and look back: even while looking, plodding slowly away. The mules break into a run when they see the cabin: Wayne cries out angrily, but their will is loosed: they thunder foolishly across the meadow, stumbling and stepping into holes. Wayne goes racing by me, spurring Dime: his saddle's creaking madly, his spurs are bouncing up and down and jingling wildly. He's riding hard, cursing, and we watch him and the mules spread out across the meadow, all of them galloping, and check our own horses severely, rein back, to keep from following.

9

Birthday Party

ECK'S THE ONE who turned me on to frozen grapes, but it's Jim Trunzler who showed me where the Locust Fork was, and it's his birthday again, Larry's too–time for the annual Locust Fork White-water Tryst. Before leaving, I go by the library and check out one of those almanac-type books, the kind that tells you what famous person was born on each day of the year, but for Larry's and Jim's birthdays, the page is surprisingly blank. A couple of dead senators, Bat Masterson, and Truman Capote. That's it. But no matter. A birthday party on the Locust Fork, even on a relatively tame day in history, is not to be missed.

I am able to slip away from my midwife of a job at three-thirty Saturday morning. Heat lightning is booming all around me, like a battlefield, as I leave. Outside Chunky, I drive without the headlights on for a while, to relieve the monotony. In Meridian I get gas, and in Toomsubsa the sun comes up, and then there is His Ozziness in Oneonta, looking surprised to see me. Little wild plum trees, and blue-and-white blossoms, line the wicked road leading in, overgrown and rocky and downhill, and it is at the bottom of this road that Ozzie is standing.

Other cars arrive, back from the Ponderosa steak house, and paddlers begin to emerge from them, walking pregnantly, hands on backs, full of ham, smiling dazedly. Green-and-black canoes, and white-and-red kayaks lie about on the riverbank like bizarrely spawning fish. We bend over them, lacing them up, flotation bags, spare paddles, coolers, and throw ropes. The woods are soft and sunny; the hum of the hair-dryer-sounding flotation-bag inflator fills up some of the quietness. We slip the boats into the water, and ourselves into the boats. It's like an invasion. There are about twenty of us; a crow flaps off, disturbed, worried. I watch for hummingbirds; sometimes you see them on this river.

It's the first real trip of the year on the Locust: I feel it needs some sort of dressing up, some acknowledgment, ornamentation.

"Picasso was born on this day in history," I feel obliged to tell Larry. But Larry is looking around, watching the river, as if that is more important.

We float on along, beneath steep bluffs whose birthday was four hundred million years ago, and beneath the Highway 79 bridge. The water is cool, 2.5 on the gauge stick and muddy from new strip-mining activity upstream. But the sun's out, with only a few clouds here and there to respect the rain forecast, and so it seems okay.

We paddle a while, and float a while. Beaver slides line the shore, and river willows, in the flat stretches, lean downstream from heavy floods now gone. We stop for lunch. Jay eats oysters, and something green: we watch, amazed.

Most of the standing waves are sitting down today; the water's low, and not angry. It is a peaceful day in history. We scout Double Trouble, and run it. Chuck films, but there is no carnage. Tom rolls his kayak at the bottom, and when he comes back up, quickly, his bright orange helmet misses the big cliff rock on the right by three, maybe four, one-hundredths of an inch. He floats on down the river, serene.

A very peaceful day in history, indeed.

I babble.

"The birchbark canoe was invented on this day, in 1601," I tell Ramona, lying.

Ramona smiles politely. Not much later I hear her asking Lucian, in a whisper, how much sleep I got last night.

The water's down, flat, normal; rock gardens are played in, and holes surfed, pools eddied; a shore bird, heron, crane, flies off, alarmed at our approach—and then we are to the falls, and things are different, it's like finding a skull or something where you did not expect it. The air above the falls is cool. It is like something from a villain movie, paddling across the current to get to the rock island; there is the knowledge that if you don't paddle, you'll just get sucked down the river and over the falls, sideways, or some embarrassing thing. Also, your canoe would probably be broken up, kind of splintered on all the rocks and things below.

We land the canoes. We get out and look.

Scouting it is like rolling up your sleeve at the doctor's office.

Tom is talking to himself. "I ran it last year," he keeps saying. He, like all of us, is pretty hypnotized by the thing: this whole river full of water falls about seven feet over this bluff ledge; the water crashes onto rocks below.

Canoe experience, canoe expertise, varies in the group.

"Probably the best bet is to try and punch through that big hole," I tell myself, and then hear Ozzie telling Larry, "Probably the best thing to do is to go through that little hole in the center." We are talking about the same place.

We continue to scout. Across the falls, through the mist, back in the trees, are fishermen. Four generations: Old, old woman, her son, his son, and his little baby, in a papoose sling. The old lady holds her pole determinedly, pointing it at the water like a metal detector. Fishless, and eighty-four. The kayakers below the falls watch her, and she watches back.

Chuck's the first in our group to go, solo, in the black Blue Hole. He braces his paddle at the top of the falls and does not move it all the way down: he glides over and down, like a feather. We are disappointed: somehow, we feel cheated. We all run it after that, and it's not too bad, because even though it's really easy, like one of those water rides at a carnival, there is still excitement, and wildness, right at the top of the falls, with all the mist and foam.

We paddle flat water, willow bends, and riffles to the take-out, against a small wind; niglets of rain splatter us about a quarter mile from the bridge, just enough to make the steep pitch of the climb below the high bridge slippery. A chain of paddlers is formed, in shifts of four, and like pallbearers of deceased nobility we carry the blue and green and red canoes—looking as out of place, being out of the water like that, and handled by that many people, as a dead fish would—and by working in shifts, four people up to the first tree, four new people taking over, up to the big boulder, four more to the little crest, and four more to the top—we are finally able to bring all fourteen boats from the river bottom far below to the top of the steep canyon. We load up, head for camp.

Campfire

The drizzle has stopped, or all but. We bathe in the frigid water below camp, change, dry our hair. Sit in a circle, a big one, beneath the rain fly. A bottle of apple schnapps is opened, the birthday toast, and the cap disappears. This distresses no one. The rain starts again, but it's okay: mellowness has descended. We're dry, and warm. Ozzie uses Ramona's knee for a pillow. Hayes uses the earth for a chair.

Another cap tumbles to the ground and is lost: peppermint this time, and again, there are no tears.

We sit, and talk, wait for it to be time to go eat.

"Let's eat," says Chuck.

"Let's dance," says Snooky.

So we sit and talk a little more. Then it is suddenly and from out of nowhere official dusk; everyone jumps up, alarmed, as if late, and rushes off, as a herd.

Hayes is startled; Hayes has not been around this crowd around dinnertime before.

"I don't know why they left so soon," he tells me. Hayes and Randolph and Jay and I are the only ones left. The entire exodus took about twenty seconds. Hayes sounds puzzled, plaintive, worried and betrayed.

So we head for Oneonta, through the farmland, in the dusk, and we pass a Methodist wedding, at a church on a hill.

It has started raining harder, steadily, when we reach Oneonta, and the Round-The-Clock Restaurant.

It's all you can eat for three dollars. The train of us stands in line, plates in hand: there are, I think, about eighteen of us. We fill our plates, our trays, and, hungry from paddling, spread out to about three or four tables, and begin to eat.

Oneonta watches, amazed.

Hayes is the first to go back for seconds; Hayes made it possible for everyone else to do so also, without embarrassment. Hayes was first. I noted this on a scrap of paper to be sure; it's a fact. Chairs scrape as others rise.

Winfred E's one of the scrapers; he goes back too, and is gone a long time. We hear, after a while, a waitress's protestations, coming from back in the kitchen, but they grow quieter and quieter, and shortly thereafter Winfred returns, beaming, with a small piece of a birthday cake topped by a few flaming, precariously perched, tiny candles.

"It was one of the cooks' birthday," he says. We sing.

And Hayes goes back for thirds.

There used to be a legend, once, about Chuck Estes. The legend was strong, and it was about his intake of chocolate pudding, and fried chicken, and cornbread, and vegetables. Iced tea, and coconut pie, and salt pork, and green beans.

When Hayes goes back for fourths, the legend becomes a glimmer. Strong men become uneasy; gentle women look away. It is not a pretty sight.

And Hayes finishes. And leans back and smiles.

And then we are off for Nectar.

They can't drink in Alabama, so they clog. Oh, it's a find, all right, Kelly's Barn is, out in the middle of the north Alabama night. Cars stretch up and down the highway, pulled off to either side, for a hundred yards. We park at the end and walk up the road, speculatively agog.

"I bet it's cock fights," says Randolph.

"Mud wrestling," opines Hayes.

There aren't any doors to Kelly's Barn: just open frames, open doorways. There are benches outside for the Young People to sit on: Nectar girls sit on these benches and talk to each other and brush their hair, and count how many boys fall in love with them. And, besides the pretty girls, there's an outhouse. It is wonderful.

We step inside Kelly's Barn, and gape.

"Wow," says Randolph.

Hayes beams, rocks back on his heels, beams some more.

"Hot damn," Hayes says, and looks up, all around. Rafters. Pews. Ceiling fans. Tin roof. Hips. Wet beads of sweat on the foreheads of the participants. They are clogging furiously, on a wooden floor, in the wooden barn. People, spectators, or maybe just resting cloggers, sip Cokes, eat popcorn. The band is up front, on a very small stage, and they're the real thing, with banjos and fiddles and dulcimers, and manure still on their boots. They're good, real good. There are lots of children, running bright-eyed and etc.; the adults smile slightly. There's a lot of noise, a lot of energy.

The more social members of our crew begin to emerge: Snooky, and Bob, and Jay, and Eve.

Hayes, and himself.

Time is not wasted. While the others dance, we begin to talk to the Nectarines, and they to us. A high school sort with a Locust Fork football shirt cross examines us, dissects us. He is intrigued with Ramona's boots. And everyone wants to know where we're from, and stuff like that, but Locust Fork is especially inquisitive: fascinated is the only word for it. He pauses, then goes into hysterics when Mike tells him he is from Louisiana. Mike is startled at the reaction, then recovers.

"Win's from Kentucky," he offers. This excites Locust Fork very much, and he calls his friends over; out of the corner of my eye, I see Win chewing slowly on a toothpick. Win does not change expression, but the toothpick snaps. He stares grimly at the cloggers.

I don't know what the Rules for Clogging are, but you can tell that there are some: you can tell by the way everyone's faces are stern and concentrated, and by the stiff, upright way in which they are holding their backs as they parade around and around in the circle that Rules do exist, and that they are to be minded.

Hayes looks like a mad stork. Even from our back pew, against the wall, we can hear his whoops, the thumps of his to-the-knee booted stomps. His elbows are lethal weapons; he spends a good portion of his dance time flapping through the dance circle backwards, eyes shut, singing face uplifted, singing loudly. Small children break formation, peel out of the circle, dive for cover. Older Nectarines stare; it is their turn for mouths to drop open. Hayes is having a good time.

And it is an athletic performance; even we, jaded Jacksonians, people from the city, are impressed, and pause, and watch. As does everyone.

The band never slows down.

It's real, real friendly. Everyone talks, is pleasant to, jokes with, even, the outside horde that has come in from out of the night, from Jackson, Mississippi. We do gawk, a little, I am afraid, but despite this I truly see only one lady, a harpy in gold earrings and pince-nez glasses and a staggering beehive hairdo, who looks as if she would like to pinch my head off. And that may well be just because I remind her of someone.

One little girl has on taps; watching her, and listening, I imagine that I can feel the floor growing warm.

For no reason, no reason at all, a man—perhaps Locust Fork's father—comes up and asks me to confirm that I am from Jackson. I tell him yes.

"I hate Jackson," he says. "I got married there, but that was the only reason."

I made a bad mistake. I get interested. Sympathizing, a little.

"Your wife was from Jackson?"

"No. But I hated it."

Oh.

"That was a daughter and two grandchildren ago. That was a long time ago."

It could go on, I realize; I slip away. Outside it is cool, like November, like April. There is a string of bare light bulbs wired across the low foggy night sky: rain coming, in a day, or less. Another band's out there, right by the doorway in a corner, practicing, warming up to take the current band's place. A group hangs around them, listening, and in the group, I see a man in jeans and cowboy boots interrogating someone else, someone with his back turned, most intensely: curious, and friendly.

"Jackson?" he says. He's talking to a drenched and wild-eyed Hayes, who has somehow made it out here from the dance floor, and looks mighty tired. "I used to drive that damn road every week," he says.

So he's familiar with it, too. And questions, questions: he wants to know how fast our canoes will go.

"Fifty knots!" cries Hayes.

Hayes is caught up, that's all there is to it. The Nectar driver nods: after watching Hayes dance, this is evidently possibly believable.

"What about the rocks?" he says. He pronounces the word like a religious entity: Rocks.

"Well, we try to miss them," says Chuck, and Hayes nods, we all nod. Of course, always, try and miss the Rocks.

But the truck driver is not so easily swayed: he is determined to see carnage.

"Well, but what happens if you do hit one?" he insists.

"Well, you tump over, and you go one way, and the boat goes the other," says Chuck.

"And then you chase it down the river?" says the truck driver.

"Right."

The truck driver leaves us at that point.

I've got to try the outhouse; I can't wait any longer. I'm really fired up, very excited.

There aren't any outhouses in Jackson.

It's down a hill, pretty steep, and my entrance is grand: the grass is slick with dew, I sort of slide down the hill and right on in. It's unoccupied.

It's illuminated; there's electricity, for the light bulb, anyway. And two rolls, extras: really quite cozy. I look all around and admire the simplicity: wood, everywhere. And the graffiti: it is so minimal that I gasp. Standing there in an outhouse in Nectar, Alabama, at about ten o'clock on a Saturday night, I am perhaps the most impressed I have ever been: Ma and Pa Kelly run a clean operation. All that youth, all that energy, and this is the only graffiti, I promise, that was in that outhouse:

SANDI LOVES BEN.
and
TERRI LOVES ???????

Seven question marks: poor Terri!

The night slides by. The cloggers keep going strong, but the paddlers fade. We drift off, dazed by the Experience, in carloads of threes and fours, leaving, no doubt, a diluted, blurring impression in the minds of Nectar about the staying power of Jacksonians.

There's not even a campfire, back on the river. Just tent zipping and feeling-good-stiffness groans. And silence, and fog, and night.

Breakfast at the Ponderosa, and a return to normalcy. Blue sky, unexpectedly, and Win stealing sips from my coffee mug, and then asking, indignantly, how I expect him to drink it when I put sugar in it. He's his usual old self, calling the waitress "dear," and getting extra grits on his plate, an extra pat of butter. At the next table, I hear Chuck, being served, say, very brightly, "Yesterday I was the last one to be served, so today I am the first"—sounding very pleased, as if his very theory on the order of the universe has been confirmed, an odd sort of Chuck-justice, and Jim lights up a cigarette. Win calls the waitress "dear" again.

The water's down a little, when we put in, but the weather's nice: a pleasant trade, not so bad. We paddle, take out at the old covered bridge not so far down the river, and then drive the damn road back into Jackson, another year older.

10

Fish Fry

THE BIG QUESTION of the afternoon seems to be this: should I take my tennis shoes and short cool athletic socks off, or should I keep them on? They're propped up on the end of the dock, atop the ice chest; I'm sitting in a rusty old lawn chair, quite comfortably, watching the sun go down, watching the lake, writing. I've got a jug of Chablis on the ice chest, and some of my kid sister's brownies. I've got one of my heavy duty goblets, about half empty now, within arm's reach, perched atop the rotting old railing of the pier; easy striking distance. I like sitting on piers. The evening is beginning to cool, and it is delicious: condensate forms on the outside of the goblet, beads up, looks pretty. I feel elegant. I am wearing my old cutoffs and still cannot decide about the shoes and socks.

It is Saturday evening; it has been a long week. In a sort of luxuri-
ant, tentative compromise, I untie my shoelaces, loosen them up a
bit, then prop my feet back up on the old ice chest. Noble ice chest. I
feel a sudden, warm, almost brotherly glow toward it, toward the
places we've been together—skiing up in the Gros Ventres of Wyoming, wind surfing down on the coast of Florida, lake touring and
walleye fishing in Wisconsin . . . and then I realize I am perhaps
sipping a little too much of the Chablis, that no one is supposed to
feel camaraderie toward an ice chest. I set my goblet down and turn
and watch the lake for a while. A dragonfly passes by, cruising,
pauses, then lights on the lip of my goblet. I shoo him away benignly.
A bead of sweat rolls down into my eye.

The month is June. I have been invited to Chuck Estes's fish fry, an
impromptu sort of thing that he just slapped together Friday afternoon, as everyone else was leaving town, bound for the coast, bound
for relatives' houses, bound for New Orleans, and Memphis and
Vicksburg and Houston. It is the weekend before the Fourth of July,
and is really the last weekend in Mississippi that we'll have before the
temperatures ease up over one hundred degrees. The bream are still
on their beds. I eat a brownie, continue to look out at the lake, and
muse on nothing.

There are seven of us. Six are out on the lake fishing. There's my
roommate, Larry, alone in his canoe, silent, studious, casting too
hard, stern-jawed; and there's Chuck, and Jim and Adrian, in the flat-
bottom boat, mellow city, sipping a beer, casting lazily, saying something light and refreshing occasionally; and then there's Sue and her
date, Eric, who have a plan, who are organized, who have one ice
chest full of tiny beefstick sandwiches and another full of cold drinks,
and who are working their way methodically around the perimeter of
the lake, counterclockwise, and who have not caught anything.

But I am being unfair. We are all unwinding, each in his own way.
Relaxing.

I decide to slip my shoes off. I can always put them back on if I
wish: it is not a big decision. You only go around once in life. And
would it be gluttonous to eat another brownie? I decide to find out.

Two more dragonflies buzz by at the end of the dock, the sun sinks
a little lower still, the lake is flat and calm and glassy now; with no
sounds anywhere except for the quiet evening sound of a mourning
dove, lazy, and I cannot help but wonder what the poor folks are

doing. Jim and Adrian, and Chuck, in the flat-bottom, disappear around a cove at the other end of the lake. It's Chuck's grandmother's lake, smallish, nameless, about four acres, and only fifteen minutes from Jackson, and pretty. There are trees all around it; it is shallow. Come around noon, in the early summer, and you can hear lone bobwhites courting, calling, whistling, in the high grown-up weeds along the fence rows. The smell of honeysuckle is almost everywhere.

A turtle surfaces out in the lake at about the eleven o'clock position, some twenty feet away; he eyes me suspiciously, and with superiority, as if questioning my authority to be out on this dock. Dry up, I think, and pour another goblet of wine. He submerges, paddles away. I notice that the heads of the nails sticking out of the dock's railing are weathered quite nicely, rather attractively, almost beautifully so, and then I tell myself that rusted nail heads on an old dock are not beautiful, not supposed to be anyway, and that I must slow down on the wine. But I cannot help but notice that there is an ornate, powder grey cauliflower-shaped curlicue of lichen on one of the rail struts, and I study it closely for a good two minutes, and I don't care what anyone says, it too is beautiful, growing on that ancient rotten weathered wood planking . . . I focus more sharply, and discover the fine mist of a spider web not far from the lichen, a study in elegance and symmetry . . . my mind recalls from musty spring days in a classroom, in college, clearly the work of the garden spider . . .

A fish, a big fish, splashes directly beneath the dock, flailing his bucket mouth at some dim-witted dragonfly, and I salivate, I truly do, but I have no fishing rod, and I look helplessly out at the tiny figures on the far side of the lake, and grimace . . . I notice another bug, not a spider, but a mayfly, delicate beautiful wisp, that flutters hopelessly around for a while and then crashes into the lake. Another fish eats him, with much relish. A minnow swims by the end of my dock, topwater, and he, too, is devoured. Nervously, I begin to wonder if maybe I am not sitting a little too far out on the dock.

Later. Activity is quiet again, and I begin to think how much I like to eat the fins, dorsal and ventral both, and tail too, deep fried in mustard batter. No one else likes the fins; if only we could catch one fish, I'm assured of the fins, nobody eats the fins. A crop duster passes by, low and slow, a biplane in the evening twilight sky, and I feel good, we really *are* out in the country . . .

Across the lake, Larry gets a strike, sets the hook, then loses it and curses loudly. I sit up with interest. Things are beginning to look up.

In my ice chest, hidden, is a three-pound pack of venison. I feel guilty, like a sinner, like I've lost my faith—I have not told anyone of this doubt, and hope mightily that I do not have to use it. A little bug, striderlike, skates across the glass of the lake not far beyond the end of the pier; I sit transfixed, watching him skate, knowing what will happen, and sure enough, just as I think it may not, there is the sudden and ominous arrival of a dark shape, below him, a slight pause, and then a tremendous splash, a gigantic splash, really, for such a tiny, tiny pinhead of a bug, and there is nothing I can do. I glance helplessly out at the tiny figures so far away, so useless . . . I am getting uneasy, growing nervous . . . There are few forced cheerfulnesses as deadly and stifling as those present at a fish fry without fish. Do not ask me how I know this, I just know it.

Chuck, my man, that crafty codger, comes in and climbs out of Jim and Adrian's boat, gets in his own, rigs up a cane pole, and I feel good all over. It is like watching Luke Skywalker climb into his spaceship, like watching Lorne Greene mount his horse, you know the fish fry is rescued now . . . Off in the distance, out on the county road, a truck goes by . . . I look down at the lake, and admire the reflections of the delicate, wispy-thin clouds that are present this sunset June evening, and think, it is a good year to be young in. I pour another glass of wine, not a very full one this time, as I am beginning to yawn.

It has been a very long week.

And the fish fry is yet to come. We need to be getting on with it, if we are to be catching any fish. The sun is flat over the trees now, in what would be alpenglow time, out West, and it's true, the willows and live oaks and sycamores and cottonwoods do begin to take on a little personality, suddenly asserting themselves with quite a bit of individual coloration, beautiful and never before noticed but now very evident hues of lovely gold, flat yellow, and generous green . . . The sun is doing that thing it does on some special evenings, sort of sitting up above a big hole in the clouds, sending golden shafting spinning beams of light down through the gap in the clouds; majestic is the word the poets use, the lake is as slick as silence, eternal, and the evening suddenly grows cool, the temperature drops five degrees— there's the bark of a dog, always the bark of a dog in the evening, from someone's farm out there, and mist begins to float across the lake.

"All right," Chuck cries lazily. His voice carries soothingly across the lake, and I look up to see him boating a fish, and hear the words come drifting across, "big bream," and I am very happy; Hot dog, I think, and to celebrate, eat another brownie, slip off my socks, grin, stretch, and am as happy as I have been in a long time. I feel like dancing on the end of the pier, throwing my arms up in the air and singing something . . . at the end of my pier little white aphids dance, swarm in circular fashion, bobbing up and down in the night dusk . . . a bass pops hard, pops loudly, out under the willow tree to my left, and the cottonwoods flush golden, suddenly taking on yet a newer hue as the sun drops a notch, and for the first time, the trees beyond the cottonwoods—the taller, greener, more lofty bull pines— come into focus, now that the sun is down below them, too . . .

A bullfrog, *Rana catesbeiana,* utters his first hoarse croak of the evening, and also, back in the trees along the coves and bays, tree frogs begin to trill. There is suddenly quite a bit of bird activity, robins and blackbirds and tweedledees of birds I've never identified before . . . What a sunset, I think, trying to compare it to something, and when the thought comes, I am ashamed: it seems suddenly cliché and unfitting, but I cannot help it, it must be the wine; so help me, the sunset looks like a painting, everything is too perfect, too made up . . . I did not think they made them like this, in Mississippi.

The bird activity has increased to the frenetic level; there must be a thousand of them calling, trying to get all their last-minute business in before sundown, I guess . . . the sun slips down under that hole in the clouds, exudes a lovely pinkish-goldish-purplish glow from behind; out on the highway a tractor-trailer growls, the bird life continues to cry, it grows cooler still, and I wiggle my toes. "Hoo!" cries Chuck, across the lake, and catches another fish. Two bats chitter overhead and swoop across the water, snapping at night insects. A dog barks, far off, a different one, and I wriggle my toes again. I am happy. It is going to be cool enough of an evening to keep the mosquitoes away. Damn, it feels good to be young, under a hundred, on a day like this. "Haw!" cries Chuck, and catches another fish, a lunker, a bass. The fish fry is progressing famously.

It is along about the fourth glass that I feel a sure and sudden pity for Sue and Eric. They are on what I suppose is their thirtieth lap around the lake, still going counterclockwise, fruitless, Eric casting like a baseball pitcher, Sue, too, gamely hurling her beetle-spin out into the great empty waters, terribly fruitless . . . I wriggle my toes some more, and try to feel really really sorry for them, but for some strange reason, am unable to, and instead am able only to admire the way their pale blue (almost turquoise) (I love turquoise!) boat is sitting on the water . . . Off on a farm somewhere, a cow lows. It is a good sound. Chuck catches another fish, I shall feast on fins.

Larry comes into shore. I am amazed that he is the first to quit. He discovers some blackberries growing along shore and begins assaulting them, dumping them into an old milk carton, hand over fist. The fish fry is really shaping up. I suddenly feel embarrassed that there will not be enough wine to share with everybody. Better to finish off the whole bottle, I decide.

"Got one!" cries Chuck. He sets the hook, arches his rod, far across the lake. Twenty yards to my left, under an old willow tree, the big bass pops again . . . Jim and Adrian, and Sue and Eric, and Larry, especially Larry, look on in chagrin. I hoot, and my laugh carries across the lake clearly, flatly, like that of a loon. I know that Larry will reprimand me when we get home, but I cannot help it; I hoot again. It feels good to laugh; the evening is quite pleasant. It has not been all that long of a week after all . . .

I am somewhere into the last glass of wine when I discover that the old rusty lawn chair in which I am sitting will rock. This is, as you can imagine, quite a pleasant surprise; the sun is down, it's solid dusk now. The frogs drone on. I rock contentedly. Some more bats chitter across the water . . . there's a mourning dove, just one, calling, sort of a reassuring sound . . . the air grows very chill . . . I am suddenly embarrassed and very aware of that unfinished last glass of Chablis resting on the dock railing; no one thinks the calls of mourning doves are reassuring—surely it is the wine . . .

No more, I tell myself, and settle back in the chair, and watch the fishermen fish, and draw my tee shirt around me, shawl-like . . . The trees around the edge of the pond have lost their significance, their collective individuality, and have gone back to being just trees again. Chuck hoots—another fish—Larry gets back in his boat and begins paddling, subtly, I can tell, over in Chuck's general direction—Chuck and Larry are brothers . . . I finish the last sip of the glass, go out to the end of the pier, do a little Scottish jig, salute where the sunset used to be, then return to my chair . . . Chuck and Larry, and Jim and Adrian, and Sue and Eric, pretend not to notice. Larry gets a strike, misses it, he's using a topwater lure, the hooks in it are much too large for this lake, I can tell him this from where I am sitting, but I can also tell he'd never believe me . . . I look at my empty wine glass and feel just full of wisdom. Again, the toes wiggle. A swift, or maybe a swallow, flies by, rocket fast, and I watch it, admiring it all the way. To the west, probably along some farmer's grainfield, some more mourning doves are still calling, and I admire this, too. Everyone comes in. We begin to clean the fish.

I can't help it: I'm a barbarian, I guess, a cretin, a heathen, but I like the smell of fish being cleaned. The smell of success. I hide my venison.

There are stars, of course; we're out in the country, we're at a fish fry, and we eat on paper plates, and there are hush puppies too. I eat all the fins I can hold, everyone is giving me their fins, and I think to myself, I am happy. Ready for next week.

11

River People

LUCIAN HILL IS a river person; he is a paddling fool. So is his wife of twenty years, Miss Ramona. Lucian's brother, Winfred E., is even worse.

This is what Winfred does every so often up in his apartment back in Kentucky: he goes to bed with all the faucets running. Kitchen sink, bathroom sink, bathtub faucet—everything. He opens them full force before turning off the lights and climbing into his sleeping bag, and beseiged by the sound of crashing water, he falls immediately and blissfully into deep, relaxed slumber. He says it helps him get to sleep when he's troubled.

The only time he's troubled is when he's been away from a river too long—five, six days.

He has no furniture: there wouldn't be room for it and all the canoes and kayaks too.

He sits in his solo saddle and uses the thwarts of his sixteen-foot Blue Hole for a table, his Phoenix Slipper is his couch, and he lays his sleeping bag out in the Mad River Explorer. Winfred is thirty-seven, just three years younger than Lucian, but he's still a bachelor.

Today, Memorial Day, we're escaping the madness of Jackson as a group—Lucian and Ramona, myself, and the ubiquitous Jim Trunzler. This is not a Sierra Club outing, not a sanctioned one anyway; it's just something we got together to do as friends. We're meeting Winfred E. in Wesser, North Carolina, at the Lost Mine campground. I ask Lucian to spell very slowly Winfred's name. Outside of a storybook, it's the first time I've ever heard of someone, a real person, being called that.

We talk and sing and eat red-hot peanuts and click the pop tops off of soda waters taken from the backseat ice chest and listen to the radio. A song by John Prine is playing: he's singing something about old rivers that just grow stronger. We're driving Lucian's new Volvo: it's a fancy automobile, gold and shiny, with a good heavy-duty air conditioner. Our green canoes glitter atop it like noble decorations, bound for Carolina. Lucian used not to travel in such style.

Lucian is big. He's an accountant for the phone company, but he's also a weight lifter. Before Lucian married and had to go to college and learn something he could make a living with, he and Winfred used to do nothing but lift weights and work on the farm and, on the weekends, canoe. The two brothers at one time owned seven canoes, six kayaks, and a beagle. No car.

They lived in Yazoo City, Mississippi. There is no whitewater in Yazoo City, Mississippi.

What they'd do is this: they'd hitchhike to wherever it was they were going. They'd watch the news at night, and if it looked like the big whitewater rivers in Georgia and Tennessee and the Carolinas were getting rain, they'd leave Yazoo City the next day. They'd carry their boats out to the county road and sit down and wait for a ride. They were handsome devils, not too badly scarred yet, and not mean-looking at all; they nearly always got a ride. Somehow Lucian would always end up carrying both his and Winfred's canoes, one slipped over each brawny shoulder, while Win held his thumb out and carried the paddles.

Also, they were so crazy about canoeing that they'd do this: they'd get up early and paddle a long stretch of river, say fifteen or twenty miles, and then shuttle back to the starting point (again hitchhiking) and run it again, by moonlight this time. They'd just use one canoe for these night runs; they'd take turns napping in the bow while the other paddled. They never turned over, they never bumped into boulders, or took on water. They claimed it was very peaceful, sleeping down in the bottom of the canoe as it hurtled down out of the mountains like that.

One year they hitchhiked up to Vermont, to compete in the try-outs for the U.S. Olympic team; they won all their races, their times were much faster than anyone else's, but for one reason or another they never went. Lucian married Ramona, and bought a car. Win moved to Kentucky, and also bought a car. Years passed, with out-standing canoe trips the only markers instead of birthdays and anni-versaries. A way of life passed with the years too—they'd never paddle again as much as they had in the old days—but they still spent a lot of time in the rapids.

It is a testimony to Lucian and Ramona's twenty-year marriage that Ramona does not know how to canoe. Today, after twenty years and perhaps three-quarters of a million miles of driving to and from the same old whitewater rivers of the southeast over and over and over, Ramona is actually going to do something other than run shuttle.

Ramona is going to solo the Nantahala; she's going to run Lesser Wesser falls. She's never really paddled before—not on a river—but she's going to give it a try. She's been practicing at the breakfast-room table; she would sit in the chair and then, like flash cards, Lucian would call out a stroke.

"J!" he'd bellow.

Ramona would J.

"Cross-bow!" he'd cry. She'd swing over to the other side and pre-tend to dip the blade sideways.

"Rocks ahead!"

Ramona would pretend to eddy out.

"Good draw," he'd tell her, and she'd actually blush with pride, as if she'd really done it.

She's frightened of water a little, yes, and of rocks and boulders and crashing foam and surf a lot, yes, but she wants very badly to be a river person like her husband and brother-in-law.

I'm not a river person; I'm still a mountain-and-desert person, I'm afraid. I have a canoe, and I'm going to paddle, but the real reason I'm going along is to eat some more of Trunz's camp cooking. Rumor has it that he has brought eggplant along again, and I overheard him whispering something to Ramona about avocado sandwiches.

I love avocado sandwiches.

We take turns driving; we take turns buying gas. It's a good feeling, riding in someone else's car, a good-running car, with a mechanic—Jim—in your midst. The confidence and feeling of security and well-being is heightened by the fact that Jim also owns a car exactly like the one we're driving; he knows it inside and out. I sit in the back seat and nod off. Birmingham blushes in a crimson sunset.

Chattanooga. Ooltewah. Ducktown, and Isabella. Finally, Murphy, N.C. It's close to midnight: we've been driving for over nine hours. (We're river people, in search of a river). The engine gears down; we enter the mountains of the Nantahala National Forest. Feathered black darkness and smelling-of-early-summer nighttime presses in, and wall the road on either side, and behind us and in front of us. The road climbs and winds, sinks and stretches before climbing again. We drive with the windows open. Off to our right, a few hundred feet below, the river roars.

The Nantahala

I'm up early, but so is Lucian: he's lifting a rather big rock up and down, repeatedly. I sit and watch for a while—neither of us says anything—until I tire of watching and go look for firewood. When I return he has finished his rock exercises and already has a fire going.

Breakfast is cooked; breakfast is eaten. It's a cool, almost cold, foggy morning down in the Nantahala Gorge; it's often like that, even in summer, because the gorge walls are so steep and high. Water trickles down the cliffs from a hundred different little seeps above our tents; gentle ferns and wildflowers are everywhere this time of year. Jim squats by the fire and flips another blueberry pancake; the sun rises, and filters down through twenty different stages of hardwood to land with a golden glow on our campsite. It's a fuzzy sort of morning, slow and sleepy. Everything seems to be either green or gold, soft looking, like a pastel. It's beautiful, and above all, relaxing.

Campers (fellow river people) walk down the road past our camp, headed for the river, walking downhill in lazy-legged plod–strides that belie their eagerness to get to the water. They pretend to be drinking in and basking in the beauty of the North Carolina summer morning, but I know they are faking it–I know what they're really thinking about is the rage of the river. Jim flips another blueberry pancake, and then puts another skillet on the fire and begins frying some sausage patties. Winfred E. drives up, bleary-eyed but smiling. He's short, and wiry, not at all like his brother. He shouts and whoops and gets out and dances around in the road when he sees us.

At this point in time, he'd been away from a river for almost two solid months. He had broken his arm over on the Chattooga earlier in the spring.

There are hugs, and handshakes, and backs are slapped. The pastel aura lifts; everything seems suddenly sharper. A thrush sings from the cliff; a blue jay flies through the trees. Winfred E. sits down and asks if breakfast is ready.

It's a funny river, I suppose. It's a little sad, really–it reminds me of watching a great powerful dog being chained to a pole, or something like that. It's a release-and-flow river. It's been dammed, for power, but each day it's released for twelve hours to keep the lake behind the dam from flooding, and to send power and water on down the road to others. It's a Jekyll-and-Hyde existence. For twelve hours, it's a meek and mild trickle; sportsmen fish in the little riffles, and you can see the stony bottom all the way across. It's a creek, not a river. It's like looking at it without its clothes on; it embarrasses us, as well as the river.

It makes up for it the other twelve hours. It's a wild thing, much wilder than it would be if it were free all the time instead of being cooped up half the day. It is this wildness that makes river people appreciate it so. They can, as the phrase goes, relate.

The water is usually turned on around nine o'clock in the morning. It's as cold as winter, coming out of the bottom of the deep lake, and it races down the gorge like it has something to prove, like it's afraid that each day might be its last. From put-in to take-out it is an eight-mile run, and is one of the finest in the East. It's a good whitewater river; it's technical, and it's high volume, but it is also pretty clean.

There aren't any sunken trees and limbs to snag and drown capsized boaters as they tumble downstream.

We wait around camp for a while, and watch the morning grow warmer—the fog lifts, leaving everything crisp looking and dripping—and then, when we feel that the first-rush crowd waiting for the release up at the put-in has gotten started, we too get in our cars and head north. We leave Win's car at the bottom, at the take-out; we all five ride in the Volvo up to the put-in. The road follows the river. Halfway there, we notice a change in the volume of the river noise. It is much louder. We pull over and peer down into the gorge. The river has changed.

For twelve hours, it is free. We get back in Lucian's car and continue on. We reach the put-in, unload the boats, and blow up the inflation bags. Ramona says nothing. I catch her adjusting her life jacket on seven different occasions. Even after she finally has it the way she wants it, she nervously continues to finger it up around the throat, like a woman feeling a pearl necklace to make sure it's still there. Her eyes are glassy, we can tell they're not seeing the soft green mountains and rocks and sky or the excitement of all the other paddlers—jeeps and trucks and cars and vans of every possible description, and people too—and Lucian pinches her behind to make her jump. She does, and yips too, and turns in outrage to see who did it. We all laugh. It wasn't that funny, but we're so excited, so tense, that we'd have laughed at anything. We carry the boats down to the water. I notice that Lucian is carrying Winfred E's as well as his own. I help Ramona tote hers down, then we come back for mine. Winfred E. has wandered over to a little gazebo-like stand the Forest Service has set up and is leaning against it, saying something to a rather attractive girl in blue-jean cutoffs and a halter top. She has long white hair, hair down to her shorts: not good canoeing material. We turn away for a moment, and when we look back, she is coming with us. Or rather, with Winfred E. Her name is Allison. She's from Missouri, we find out. No, she's never canoed before. Yes, she'd like very much to try—is Winfred sure there's enough room? Winfred says he guesses there is.

We're in the water. Those first few cold splashes as you run out into the shallows, push off, and then jump in; the first couple of paddle strokes where it feels like you're not doing any good, like you're paddling in molasses, and then they begin to catch, and the canoe starts to move forward, quickly, strongly . . . the canoe itself sings down the river, like a thing released from a dam too.

We feel the same.

One of the best things about the Nantahala is this: there is a good set of rapids right around the corner from the first put-in. It's called Patton's Run, and it's a good idea not to dump in it, because it'll be a long day. The sun never strikes the river straight-on for very long; it's always at least partially in the shadows, and the water's very cold. Also, it is a very long stretch of whitewater—you'll probably be washed down for as far as a quarter of a mile before it flattens out enough for you to crawl out and empty your boat.

But Ramona handles it perfectly; so do Winfred E. and Allison, and the rest of us. It's over incredibly quickly, in just a few seconds it seems, and we eddy out into a still place and gasp and pant and all try to talk at once. Our hearts race.

It's not the best stretch of rapids on the river, but it's one of my favorites: it's sure a nice way to start a Memorial Day weekend.

We're in the shadows; we're wet from the spray, and shivering. Also, we're pumped with adrenalin. We wheel out into the mainstream and push on. We race down the river like snow skiers coming down a mountain. The boats rise and chop and crash against the waves; we scream and shout and laugh and dodge through the rocks; the boats and the river are holding a wild and joyfully angry communion together, and we're lucky enough to be caught in the middle. Lucian shouts out instructions from time to time to Ramona, but most of the time, I can tell, she does not hear them: the river is too loud, too jealous. No matter: she appears to be holding her own. Jim races past me, stroking hard. His red beard is soaked with river spray, and he is grinning madly. He does not notice me. There is an odd shine in his eyes.

I fall in a good distance behind him; I try to follow his turns, to avoid the rocks and really bad waves, but it is not until the second stretch of hard rapids that I begin to suspect he is aiming into the tallest waves on purpose rather than trying to avoid them. I draw out to one side and strike out on my own.

That's another good thing about the Nantahala: there's always plenty of people, yes, but there's also plenty of room. And traffic is fast: if you don't like it, just wait, and it will blow past you in a second. You can go where you want to, do what you want: the banks on either side, and the fact that you can't go back upstream, are your only boundaries.

Actually, when you analyze it, it's a little surprising: you really only have one choice of where to go, and that's downstream. And yet it seems like you've got more freedom than you've ever had in your life: those banks on either side, and that wall of water pushing down on you from behind are so far from your mind that they're not even comprehensible–all you can think about is the wild joy of going down, down, down the river, hard out, all the way to the end.

If you focus on the right things, and ignore the others, you can find wildness and freedom anywhere, I am convinced.

I did not notice the road that ran above us a few hundred feet, following the river; I did not notice the awesome rock quarry we passed, cut into the side of a mountain, with tiny yellow cranes scratching weakly at its base while it waited patiently for them to finish and go away with whatever it was they came for. I did not notice the rafts and inner tubes and sometimes overall carnival-like atmosphere of all the river people on the slower stretches. I focused instead on the stretch and pull of my muscles and the paddle pulling water, and the sleek way the canoe carried itself downstream, and the caddisfly larvae in the shallow pools, and the wonderfully shocking coldness and cleanness of the water, and the green and pink of the mountain laurels, and the cold clean smell that all river canyons have in their shadowy parts, and I saw not one person go by that I didn't honestly like.

In Jackson, sometimes, I'll walk an entire city block, to the bank and back, and never smile at anyone.

In some places, it is true, it is easier to focus than in others.

We had lunch in a meadow, up off the river in a wide spot where the gorge stretches to a width of perhaps five miles. There were a few other people up in the meadow picnicking also, looking down on the river, but most of them were continuing to bomb on down the river; most of them probably didn't even see the meadow.

It's good to bomb down the river, that's the best way, but for sure if you take little breaks then inevitably they'll help you rest up so when you do get back on the river you can go one hundred percent again.

Bombing is fine, but if you're going to do it, you need to do it right. You need to go one hundred percent. Even if this means doing something as sinfully pleasurable as taking a break to picnic in a North Carolina riverside meadow. There was dark beer, and potato chips, and a semidamp blanket to sit on. There were avocado sandwiches. I ate three of them, and lay back in the warm sun and felt my stomach. I felt happy.

You would not believe what a wizard Trunz is when it comes to food. The sun was warm on my face. There wasn't any wind. I closed my eyes. Everything seemed to hang suspended, frozen: crouched and ready to go, yet also motionless, like a child playing red-light green-light. Even sounds seemed frozen; it was as if Everything was waiting for Something. The moment hung heavy as ore for a few seconds, then sighed and moved on. I sat up and watched it leave. I was ready to go one hundred percent down the river again. I looked at my fellow river people and could tell they were too.

Also, I could tell this: that they too had felt the odd moment. It wasn't eerie, it was just puzzling, like a phenomenon, like one of those secrets of nature that you glimpse only every so often—a north-flowing river, an anomaly of gravity, an albino elk—little things She shows you only so often, just to keep you in awe, or maybe just to reward you. We chose to view it as a reward. We grinned but said nothing of it; that would have spoiled it. We pretended we hadn't seen it, so as not to startle it.

Beautiful things like that frozen-time moment embarrass easily: startle them, or study them too closely, and they might not come back. We chose just to appreciate it, not analyze it, and then we cleaned up our avocado peelings and folded the blanket and went back down to the river.

Campfire. Much like the one so many years ago (was it only seven?) around which I first heard stories about Jim Bridger, about Jed Smith. I'm in the mountains again, oddly so, though who'd ever have dreamed then they'd be the tame mountains of the East? Not I, I'd have said, had someone seen into the future.

The sparks don't pop the same, the forests don't smell the same, even the pull of gravity and sigh of the wind doesn't feel and sound the same, but the camaraderie is exactly identical, almost eerily so. This puzzles me; I muse on it at length as the others toast and cheer Ramona, who successfully and even aggressively ran Lesser Wesser with grace and beauty.

The Chattooga

It's like a graduation; it's as if we're saving the best for last. It's up in the mountains of the Georgia-South Carolina border; driving over early Sunday morning, we pass through Rabun Gap, the place where the high school students compile all the *Foxfire* books. It's Appalachia at its finest: stocky-legged dairy cattle standing firmly in hilly fields of soft green, and listing ancient wooden hay barns, and split-rail fences and old rounded mountains that are choked over by trees of a thousand different ancestors.

The Chattooga is one of the officially approved member rivers in our country's National Wild and Scenic River System—fifty-one miles of it is included in this category—and is (with the exception of the Snake, the Salmon, the Feather, the Virgin, the Madison, etc.) the most beautiful river I've ever seen in my life. It looks almost western, with its broad rushes and ledges and riffles, and its angry roars in the loud places, and with all the boulders that line the shores, and beyond that, the pine-studded mountains. The air is warm and dry, and the mountains are the biggest I've seen yet. From where we put in, we can see Mt. Rabun Bald, 4,696 feet.

The elevation down in the valley in the town I went to school in out west is 4,492 feet.

The water here is warmer than in Nantahala Gorge. We launch in a quiet place, and float. Upstream, a man and a pack horse materialize from out of the old forest. The horse paws the river with a hoof, tentatively, then the man nudges him on. There is no other sound exactly like the clop of a pack horse's hooves as it crosses a shallow ford. We look back and watch, and listen. It is a special sound, as special for us as was yesterday's odd and frozen moment at the picnic in the meadow.

River people seem to know how to see these things; they know how to tell what is special, and what to look for. What to focus on. It strikes me in a flash what the criterion is for determining if something is special: If it's not found in Jackson, it's probably special. Time doesn't hang frozen in Jackson, not ever, and you never hear the sound of horse's hooves crossing a shallow rocky river, either. In great thirsty gulps we drink in the horse and rider, watch until they disappear, then we turn and start down the river. The sun is warm, even hot; the smell of Coppertone mingles with the scent of sun-dried pine straw up in the dark and steeply forested mountains. Overhead, a hawk wheels. In front of us, a fish splashes. We are almost cautious on this quiet stretch of river; it is almost like entering a cathedral, it is so beautiful. Is it all right? Can we come in?

Yes the river answers.

Dick's Creek Falls is the first trouble spot. It's loud, and it's high; there is the typical calm before a waterfall, then a two-foot drop into a churning, frothing little pool, then a 120 degree turn to the right to go down a chute of whitewater that carves its way through rocks. The chute is perhaps a foot wider than the canoe. There is zero room for error. At the end of the chute is another drop, about four feet, at the bottom of which you must turn back 120 degrees to the left or be dashed up onto more rocks. Ramona and Lucian and Jim decide to portage. Winfred E. decides to run it. Allison decides she wants to go home. Regretfully, Winfred E. changes his mind.

I do not portage. I am seized with a sudden, crazy, death wish: I want to run Dick's Creek Falls. I want to show off.

It is not that I am a better paddler than any of them—I'm not. It's just that here's my chance to be a whitewater hero. If I run it, and no one else even tries, I've got nothing to lose. I may spill, but there's no one else to compare my run to, so it won't look bad. It will be assumed that anyone would have spilled. I'll have no competition.

At the very worst, I reckon, I will break a bone or lose a tooth or bloody a nose. But at the very best . . . The thought of running Dick's Creek Falls successfully has such dreamlike qualities about it, such potential for euphoria, that I feel almost obliged to try it. I push off into the current and begin paddling for the falls. Behind me, everyone else shouts and cheers and urges me on. I notice that time has frozen again: up ahead of me the falls—they stretch all the way across the broad flat hot river—look like a painting, and I feel like a tiny intruder on the canvas.

I decide at the last second, as I am perhaps two feet away from the lip, that I do not want to run Dick's Creek Falls after all. But time has thawed; I am going forward much too fast to stop, much too fast to hang frozen for even a second. The falls spring up and snatch at me greedily and toss me gleefully into the rocks; the canoe bumps, spins around, and carries me down the chute backwards. I hit the next wall of rocks and fall out of the canoe. The terrible sweet surge of water hurries me down the rest of the way, as if I have ventured into a sacred place and must be evicted immediately, and then spits me and my canoe out into the river below. Someone throws me a rope; I grab it and they pull me in. They're grinning; they're glad they portaged.

Maybe next year, I think. We walk downstream a way and pull my canoe out and empty the water. I climb in and we start back down the river. The sun is hotter than ever. Behind us, Dick's Creek Falls continues to roar, laughing, and waits for the next whitewater hero. My heart does not stop racing until we are around the bend.

We fare a little better at The Keyhole. It's another waterfall, except there's only one spot you can run it or you'll slam into a big boulder that stretches all the way across the river. If you miss the keyhole, you'll hit the rock.

No one misses the keyhole. We scrape past on the right of the rock, coming so close that we can feel its coldness as we pass by, but no one hits it.

At 8-Foot Falls, we all get an adrenalin rush as our canoes sail out, out, out over the edge before nosing down into the river below. It's quite a sensation, going over 8-Foot Falls solo: it's like driving a car off a cliff, like jumping out of an airplane.

After 8-Foot Falls, it gets slow. Much flat water; much paddling, and much lazing around and drifting. There is no beer drinking. Bull Sluice lies ahead. Bull Sluice is to solo canoeists what the Hindenberg was to aviation safety.

The thing to watch out for at Bull Sluice is the ender.

In whitewater jargon, an ender is often something that will end your life: a hydraulic whirlpool, a giant boulder, an undercut ledge you can be slammed under and trapped beneath; it's also the action of a kayak going straight up into the air, sometimes on purpose, sometimes not, when it gets into one of these trouble spots. The kayak stands on end. The ender at Bull Sluice is all of these things. It's a flat, sharp-edged, horizontal wedge of rock that juts out over the second waterfall (Bull Sluice consists of two drops: the first one, a brawling, violent thing, and then the second one, at a right angle perhaps ten yards downstream from the first one). Blocking the exit over the second waterfall, blocking the exit to safety and applause (dozens of people are always picnicking up on the boulders, watching the martyrs) is the flat-edged undercut giant ender called Decapitation Rock. Theoretically, if after surviving the first fall, there's a tiny opening on the right you can sneak through to get over the second one. Miss it, and the ender gets you. You may be sucked under the ledge and trapped, you may be slammed into the boulder's side, breaking numerous important bones, or you may get caught up in your canoe and roll around and around at the bottom of the second waterfall, like a hamster on a treadmill, until you drown.

The best way to get out of a hydraulic, if you get trapped in one and are still conscious, is not to fight it—you'll never be able to swim out of it, it's much too strong—is to dive down to the bottom of the river and then swim out away from it, swimming along the bottom. That's where the hydraulic trapping forces are weakest, that's how almost all the people who have escaped hydraulics have done it.

We pull up into the shallows, well upstream, and hike downriver to scout it. We overhear one of the picnickers telling another picnicker about a girl in a kayak who missed the right turn into the second waterfall last week and crashed into Decapitation Rock. "Broke her face," the first picnicker says, matter-of-factly. We all decide to portage.

All of us but one. I'm still remembering Dick's Creek Falls; I'm still pining to be a whitewater hero. I still want to earn the respect of these water people. I've driven six hundred miles for a three-day weekend, passed up a chance to go out West, and it's going to be another six hundred miles back. I know as sure as anything that if I don't make a run at Bull Sluice, I'll be regretting it within twenty-four hours of my leaving. Wondering if I could have done it after all. Berating myself for not even having tried. I sit on a boulder and study the rapids for many minutes. I try to push back the thought that I am not a strong swimmer.

Swimming is for people who fall out of their canoe.

Ramona and Lucian watch me watch the river; Winfred E. wanders downstream to meet new friends, while Lucian coils the throw rope he has brought along. Jim stations himself by the second waterfall with his camera. "You gonna die," he cries up to me gleefully. He thinks it is great fun. I frown and turn and go back upstream, up into the shallows, and climb into my canoe. I feel a little dizzy, a little giddy. Subconscious hyperventilation, coupled with a massive adrenalin influx. I stroke out into the center of the river, and allow the canoe to drift along down toward the distant falls. The afternoon sun casts a bronze glow on the falls and spectators up in the boulder field ahead; from this distance, everyone seems quite tiny and insignificant. Up in the pines on the left side of the river, up on a steep and shadowed slope, some blue jays are scolding something. They are paying no attention whatsoever to the lone figure in the green canoe that is floating downstream. The current quickens. I can see some of the spectators' heads turning; some of them are pointing at me. The river is wide; I have it all to myself, I am center stage. The water begins to rumble and froth and slap at the boat in angry little whitecaps. I realize with a grim sort of triumph that I'm now in water sufficiently fast and wild enough that I can no longer turn back. No matter how badly I wanted it, there's no power on earth that could keep me from going over the falls now. I'm committed.

Trunz makes the eggplant that night. He has all of us working on it, cutting, grating, dicing, and chopping. He's using eleven different kinds of cheese; I didn't know there were that many kinds in existence. It's going to be the great eggplant pizza of 1983: he's going to bake it atop a huge saucer of his homemade sourdough bread, wrapped in foil and placed in the coals. We watch it cook and talk about some of everything while we wait. It's nice to be camped around a fire, waiting on food after a hard day's paddling–much nicer than waiting back in Jackson for a pizza there. (As if they'd have eggplant anyway!) Jim begins telling Winfred and Allison a joke I've already heard; I tune it out and think about what I would be doing if I hadn't come on this trip with Jim and the Hills. It is an uncomfortable thought, but I study on it anyway. It's a thought that needs defining.

I'd be in the mountains, and I don't mean the ones I'm in now. I'd be in the big ones–the ones west of the Mississippi, not east. It is spring up there on the Divide, springtime at its finest, and yet I've passed up a chance to drive up there for a three-day weekend, and have chosen instead to come to the Nantahala. It is the first time such a thing's ever happened.

It's been five years; does one finally learn to adjust, and learn to live away from the mountains? After a certain period of time, does one no longer love the aspen and the glaciers with all his heart and all his soul?

I think not. John Colter went back. Jed Smith went back, and so would have Jim Bridger if he'd been able to see his way. I will too, someday, there's no doubt about it.

But when? Other than $40,000 a year, what's stopping me? Is it the beauty of Jackson? Is it Jim Trunzler's eggplant pizza?

Again, I think not. I do not know what it is. I will have to study on it some more.

The Ocoee

It's Monday morning; it's right at dawn. I've been up for about ten minutes; I'm watching Lucian's tent to see if he comes rolling out and starts lifting rocks again like he's been doing the last couple of days, but so far there's been no movement from the tan two-man Eureka. Surely he's not sleeping through his workout. Not on the morning that Jim is supposed to run the Ocoee.

It's a pleasant enough sounding name for such a fierce river. It makes the Nantahala, and even the Chattooga, look like rivers of cold honey.

Standing up on a cliff, looking down at the Ocoee, you actually get dizzy, watching it race by so fast.

Sometimes there are standing waves on it that are six feet high. You see very few canoeists on the Ocoee; it is almost exclusively a haunt for the lighter, slippier kayaks.

You make a mistake on the Ocoee in a kayak, and (theoretically) all you have to do is roll back over. But make a mistake in a canoe – blink one eyelid and not the other, inhale when you should have exhaled – and likely as not you'll be pitched out into the current and washed helplessly downstream over a washboard maze of boulders for however long that particular stretch of rapids lasts. No one can swim out of the rapids on the Ocoee; the only thing you can do is just ride them out and hope it's not a long stretch. Good luck.

The best strategy, of course, is not to turn over.

Once, during the night, I was awakened by the sound of someone having a nightmare; someone was screaming in the night.

It sounded like it was coming from Jim's tent.

You've got to be good to run the Ocoee in an open boat. I'm not good enough. I'm not even brave enough. I'm good for one run; I'll run any rapid I see, or at least try, as long as there's still water waiting below, but the Ocoee is different: it is one long rapid. The run Jim is going to do is about five miles: it should take him about an hour, counting turnovers and rest stops. Then we'll load up and head back to Jackson.

In the parking lot at the put-in, the atmosphere is a little different from the Nantahala. It's a little more professional, a little more low key. The excitement's still there, but there is not the feeling that somewhere in the background, a calliope should be playing. And everyone is lean and hard: no softies here. Smiling, but lean and hard. It is a parking lot full of athletes. They look with athletes' undisguised admiration at Jim as he unloads his canoe. Respect. His is the only canoe in the parking lot.

Lucian's good enough to do the Ocoee in an open boat, but Ramona won't let him. Winfred E. and Allison are frightened of it, and I, I have learned my limitations. The five of us are going to be shuttle bunnies; we'll bring the cars from the put-in to the take-out. It's usually not a very glamorous job, driving while everyone else is paddling, but today we're delighted to have it.

Occasionally, rocks and tree limbs are swept down the Ocoee. You can hear the muted underwater sounds they make as they strike other, more permanent, rocks. It is a sound that can only be described as the river clacking its teeth.

The sun is warm; the river is crowded. With a man on each thwart, like Sherpa porters we carry Jim down to water's edge. He sits atop his solo saddle like a benign king and smiles and nods at all he passes. His canoe is stuffed with flotation: inflated bags of air fill every available space, as much to keep water out as to increase stability. He takes a few deep breaths, rubs his beard as if to reassure himself that it's still there, then salutes us and shoves off. He's a big man, but as we watch the green canoe bob out into the crashing waters, both he and the boat look tiny, almost ridiculously so.

With the same tingle-feeling that good eager quarter-milers hear at the crack of a gun, we turn and run up the hill to the cars. It's our plan to stop at every bend in the road along the way and take pictures and wave at Jim and, if necessary, throw him a rescue line.

He is waiting for us at the first bend, having beaten us there. He is drenched; he is pulling his canoe up on shore to empty it. It is full of river water. He dumped on the first rapid, and was flushed all the way down to this point. He is breathing hard, and grinning a little, but he is also shaking his head in wonderment.

"Whew," he says.

We help him empty his boat. There's not much we can say. We grin too, but we're all a little worried. Ramona frowns and several times starts to say something. Kayaks, black and yellow and red and orange, skate by like wasps: hovering, dancing, playing, popping in and out of crashing waves like taunting children. The sun beats down so very hotly; it makes sweat run into our eyes and plasters our hair damp against us, and we're not even doing anything. The air is dry, and smells of warm pine needles. Jim adjusts one of his knee pads that has been knocked askew—there is a purple bruise on his thigh the size of a baseball—and gets back in the boat. We turn and run back up the hill. The next stop will be Table Saw Rapids.

We get to Table Saw long before Jim. We sit down in the boulders and check the throw rope and focus our cameras—he'll come around a bend, and the Saw will be waiting—and take our shirts off and feel the sun glance off the water and brown us. And though it seems almost immoral to do it, to risk spoiling such a perfect mood, I try once more to wrestle with the question that eluded me last night: Will the pain of being separated from the high country eventually lessen, and in time maybe even disappear, like a wound covered over with scar tissue? I seemed very near the answer. Up above me, trucks and cars zoom past, some coming, some going.

It's a different sensation, watching someone else navigate a rough stretch of rapids as opposed to running it yourself. You can see his mistakes, and second guess, and nod approval, whereas when you're running it yourself everything tends to blur and flash by, and if you're concentrating intently enough, by the time you're out of it you can't even remember how you did it, not the exact step-by-step sequence anyway.

We crouched on the boulders and watched and winced as each time Jim leaned back and recovered after a near capsize; we tensed and watched him go left, right, left, right, picking his way down through the chutes in fast motion. Once, he had the canoe almost on its side, like a car on two wheels. He corrected, though; he slapped a high-water brace over the side, pulled back up, and missed hitting a rock by perhaps six inches. He sailed past it, into new trouble. The rock watched him go, disappointed.

We got several nice pictures of Jim running Table Saw. After it was over, he pulled over to the shore and sat there, breathing hard. We waved at him—he was a long way downstream—and clambered back up the hillside to the cars and headed for Diamond Splitter.

There were a lot of cars parked along the road above Diamond Splitter. We passed a car with a bumper sticker that said "Wild Water—Second Only to Wild Women." Another one warned us that that car stopped at all river crossings, while a third asked us if we had hugged our kayaks today.

It's a love affair, there's no other word for it, that these people have with their rivers. Imagine: comparing a river to a woman, and hugging a boat!

I've compared a sunrise over the Pecos Wilderness to an eloping lover; I've caressed the bark of aspen and thought how it was like a woman's shoulder. Are river people the same as I? Are rivers as wild as mountains; can I be as free in Jackson, Mississippi, as I was in Utah? More trucks and cars whiz by; so many people! Jim comes around the bend, blowing and going, like a runaway freight train. He smokes over an insignificant four-foot drop, skims over a second three-foot one, and points his canoe straight into the center of the boiling green waves. They stand up and rear back and strike at him; he blows through them like an entire football team blowing through that paper they stretch between the goal posts at halftime. He is wearing that crazy-eyed Viking grin again, the one that makes me think he is not seeing us.

I have a favorite short story, by Carson McCullers, entitled "A Tree, A Rock, A Cloud." It's about an old man who collars a young boy and gives him a lecture on how men should love. "They fall in love with a woman. . . . They start at the wrong end of love," he says. "Son, do you know how love should be begun? . . . A tree. A rock. A cloud."

Perhaps I did not start with the rock; perhaps I skipped a step somewhere, and fell in love with the mountains before I was ready.

Perhaps if I had learned to love people as well as nature, they wouldn't bother me as much by merely being around. Lord knows there are enough of them around down here in the flatlands. Not only river people, but skyscraper people, stock market people, banking and finance people—not just cloud people, but rock and tree people too.

There's more rapids; there's more camera stops. Jim handles each new challenge aggressively, successfully, and when he finally comes off the river we have a cold beer waiting for him. It's fun to shake his hand; a congratulatory handshake is so different from a nice-to-meet-you.

It's truly not an easy thing, running the Ocoee in an open boat like that.

So I'm going to be like the River People; I'm going to make a stand a little while longer, and be aggressive, rather than run away every time things get a little tough, and I'm going to try to stay put in Jackson for a while. Until I can leave without having to say that it defeated me, that it broke my spirit and ran me off. I'm going to canoe the Nantahala more often, spend a lot of time backpacking in the Black Creek Wilderness Area, even if it's not as pretty (to me) as Ruth Lake and the Madison River. I'm going to try to find wilderness in people as well as nature, in friends like Jim Trunzler and his crowd, and maybe we'll even cook hamburgers out in our backyards from time to time and listen to the summertime sounds of civilization, of lawn mowers down the street and children in the evening, while we plan our next trip. I'm going to confront this business of living in the city with a little more determination, with what they call a Better Attitude, and I'm going to learn to focus on the right things in order to get by. In order to defeat the madness of Jackson.

If it's wild to your own heart, protect it. Preserve it. Love it. And fight for it, and dedicate yourself to it, whether it's a mountain range, your wife, your husband, or even (heaven forbid) your job. It doesn't matter if it's wild to anyone else: if it's what makes your heart sing, if it's what makes your days soar like a hawk in the summertime, then focus on it. Because for sure, it's wild, and if it's wild, it'll mean you're still free. No matter where you are.

12

First Snow

THE WEST LOOKS different when you get older. There is not the
audacity to suggest it is the Rockies themselves that are changing.
1968 can be no different from 1986 to a mountain. The dogs and I
left on a Saturday to go meet the snow: a Saturday in late September.

I bought a new knife. I'd lost the old one. It was only ten-some-
thing, but is a good one. I sliced off a section of my finger with it,
peeling an apple while driving. My fingerprints are altered. I have a
new identity. This pleases me enormously as I pass through Lubbock
in my borrowed truck. I feel stealthy, wild, cunning, free. The cashier
at the Dairy Queen's drive-through window does not understand my
happiness, I can tell.

All the years are different, and this one yet again, but more so. The older you get the more time you have. You have learned, mostly, what to waste your time on: what will bring you the most pleasure.

"Hounds?" asks the cashier at the Dairy Queen. She means Homer and Ann. They are puppies—sisters—black-and-tan, orphans. Another wrinkle in the years: first time I've had dogs. We're all headed West. To see snow, see it fall, for the first time this year.

"Yes," I tell her. They have long whiskers and dark eyes and are the most beautiful hounds in the world. She will never see them again. They will leave a lingering memory in her mind.

The wind is blowing from the north and west, and wet: purple, high plains. Lubbock is more Denver than it is Houston. No one knows that road as I do.

It is about my third year with the new tent. The old one, pup-style, blew out of the back of the truck one windy night as I raced to Fort Worth, from whence I would *fly* to Salt Lake, and rent a car. Even three years ago, I was always in such a hurry. I can't tell you what a mistake that was. The new tent is blue and humpbacked, like a dolphin, with little gold skeletal ribs—shock-corded, they call it—that snap together with the firm clinking sound of a martial arts weapon, and I distrust it still. There will never be another pup tent. This one has some miles to go to earn its keep. It is so modern: it is so different.

The western part of the United States: (rocks no one has ever picked up) the colors are better out there, in the fall. I am not talking about the oak and aspen, (box elder, cottonwood), aspen, aspen—I mean the skies, rocks, grass, cattle, fields, roads.

My hounds' eyes, trying to figure out why it has gotten so cold so quickly. Trying to figure out what cold even is. It is not cold. There is light frost in the mornings, but the fires and sun have kept them warm. They just think it is cold.

I have built fires everywhere: they could measure my life as well as anything. Sage fires are good to write by. Other fires pop. Cedar keeps you warm, makes you sneeze, may be king. Aspen is too pretty to burn, but smells good, if you are camping with someone else and they decide to burn the aspen. Fir was put here for fires. Pine. Even in winter, sitting on the rotten log by the fire, the bugs will come out of it, waking up, hatching, fooled by the warmth, to be surprised by the snow. It is good to run to the first snow of the year, pack the truck and drive to meet it, rather than waiting, sitting; a weak sort of ambush, and not befitting at all. Oh yes dear we may get snow tonight, and will you pass the potatoes. Snow, with a little s.

You know this is wrong, and not the way to do it. Of course the year's first snow deserves accolade, and is a thing to strive for, to welcome, to meet at least half way.

These fires, and changes: I used to write with pencil, on yellow pads. For a few years then it had to be ballpoints, in parchment diary books, and these are still convenient to fit in a coat pocket, a glove box. Of late I have declared felt-tip pens the answer, the perfect flow, but then, too, they dry out too quickly when writing by the fire, flecks of ash and stick fly up and clog them up, bring them down, gum them wordless, on these camping trips. So I am searching, still. Perhaps blood, traced on (dead) bark. Five or six words a year: well chosen, made beautiful by the exclusion of all the others.

More on fires, headed north, to meet the snow. I am in the habit of picking up the logs I've gathered but haven't burned. I hurl them back into the woods, in different directions. Some pieces I take to a certain area and place: cover with grass, somewhat, and sprinkle with leaves. Forgive the primitive instincts. They grow stronger with age. [You know more. You feel more]. When I am putting wood on the fire, if there is a dried or colorful lichen on it I peel it off and toss it free. It would be hard to estimate if this is of use to anything other than my peace.

Somewhere along the way the Visa card is misplaced. Lost? Stolen? I have an envelope with some dollars and coins in it: that will have to do. I suspect that I discarded it on purpose. Sometimes I forget things entirely. Others I remember forever. The Visa card stirs nothing in me, no recollections. From here on it will be straight-up and cash. I will pay for something, and get it. Or the other. The future has just been taken out of the trip. I think I lost it on purpose.

I like Las Vegas, N.M. I buy eggs there; potatoes, bread, butter, chicken, puppy chow. Out of the first front now, the Lubbock one, and into blue sky. Modest temperatures. No telling, though. These things can change quickly.

I turn off on a dirt road and travel up along a stream and stop and get out and let the puppies play, and eat. I drink some of the cold river with my Sierra cup. It is old and heavy and spacious. I had it when I had the tent. It is from the sixties and seventies, when my calves were larger. It makes the pack heavy. It loses heat instantly: makes your soup chill, your hot chocolate cold. The only good thing it does is make river water taste almost, very very close, the way it was in the river. It does this well. I keep it, despite my calves. The lighter, newer insulate cups are good, too, but they remind me of the tinny, hissing propane cooking stoves. I'm not saying these are immoral, either, or wrong—certainly no more so than my wood smoke—or anything like that. I am not better than the people who use them. I merely like to build fires, and I have not changed yet.

Taos. Pan-frying steak, making gravy. A something in the air. The light a filter on the fields below: evening. I burn my right thumb and forefinger on the skillet: instant blistering and torn skin. A newer identity, yet. Soon I will not be able to write for all the bandages. Was there never a trade-off for freedom? The steak is good.

Fires are lives. They will go down without change, care, and addition. All fires need more wood. Cold weather makes fires seem more full, more useful: it gives purpose to the fires. It makes the fires necessary. I am glad there is cold weather each year. It is just me and it is like the lichen thing but I always feel that I should at least go meet it.

Magpies. Sage. Woodfires. Navajo. Getting nearer. West of Taos—Chimayo—I stop for a walk. The hounds leap out and run off into the brush. Then yelping. Blue sky. I run down to the noise; they are pinned to the ground, both of them flopping, trying to get up, unable to, anchored to the ground—a coyote trap? But it is only tar, dumped there by a road crew, a pool of it. I pull them out. They run off through the sage, picking up ridiculous moon-boots of accretion: grass, weeds, straw, sticks. They are confused by it, running in all directions, splay-legged, drawing their oversized feet up high to their chests like trotting horses; each time a foot hits the ground it picks up more stuff. They are only puppies. It is funny. I am relieved. Things could be so much worse.

The air tastes thin and like the thing that will make you live to be a hundred. I drive back to Chimayo and sit on the sidewalk on the main and only street and, with a plastic jug of gasoline, begin to clean them off in the bright sunlight. People passing both ways slow down and stare. I am in my jeans and an old soon-to-be-abandoned sweater. There is several days' worth of beard. The hounds writhe, twist, try to get free, not understanding. I am patient. I will get to the snow when I meet it. It does not matter where I get to it. Only that I am trying, making the effort, making the time I can when I can: stopping for brief walks, cleaning the dogs, watching a river for a while – the unnecessary stops are okay. I am still moving more than I am not.

Leadville, two days later. Storms predicted. Two beers and enchiladas, at three-thirty in the afternoon, at the best place in the world for this, never mind the name. I've read up on my ethics, and know that's the way to destroy a thing. It may not have even been Leadville.

Windy as stink, coming back out: wind coming down out of the mountains, and cold; the dogs have to ride in the cab.

Night. Still driving. Hurrying now. Full moon.

A fire and a campsite in a place I've never been. The way the coals rumble with light when the wind blows across them is as close to the way life is as anything I've seen yet.

I turn left at Steamboat Springs: head for Utah. All day I see antelope. A lengthy picnic on a river, on a bluff looking down. Near dusk, I turn up a gravel road, and follow it until dark, then get out and put the tent up, hunt for wood with a flashlight, feed the dogs. I start the fire and look up at the stars, but there aren't any: low clouds, and windy. The dogs and I are waiting. We drove about eight hours today. It's very cold, and we're high: about ten thousand feet.

It begins to come down: white, and new, and the start of something big out here, winter in the Rockies. I always forget how quiet it is. We sit by the fire and watch it snow on us until the woods are whitened, reborn, begun again. Unzipping the tent for bed has the good sound to it, that we are the only ones, the snow and us.

Falling asleep is like knowing there is someone outside that understands you better than you know yourself: that quietness, that continued falling. It will not stop soon; the winter of it will not change.

13

Strawberries

I HADN'T SEEN Lucian in two years, and the first thing I do when I drive up is slip the clutch and lurch into the back of his new car. I didn't know it was his; it was an accident.

He stands on Jim's porch with his hands on his hips and looks at what happened.

"Good to see you," he says finally. But here is the good part: he means it.

It's eight hard and flat hours to the river in Arkansas. Before we leave, there are birds singing, and bees and honeysuckle and patches of light in Jim's and Larry's front yard, dogs barking in the neighborhood, and the mailman comes through the bushes sifting and sorting envelopes: that time of day. Larry and Jim, and Lucian, and myself, in shorts and sandals; we all shake hands, and transfer canoes and then leave, bumping up and down on the road into the center of Jackson, to pick up Ramona. The mailman continues on with his job, but not us.

Ramona steps out of the building as we pull into the back parking lot, and it is as smooth as a crime, the kind on TV where they synchronize their watches. She steps in the van.

Lucian's changing, slowly. And Jim tells me, driving, that the river is changing: that every year, it's different. Jim has an eye and a memory for every stretch of any river, and he says that on the Buffalo, annual spring floods will pick up certain gravel shoals—once a hundred feet long—and scour them away, so that perhaps an island on which you one year had lunch, will, the next year, be completely gone, with flat clear still water over where it was. Maybe crows will be flying over its absentness. Maybe they will be calling.

This is Jim's and Lucian's and Ramona's sixteenth year to paddle the Buffalo in April. I want you to know that a not so very short time ago Lucian would have done something retributive, fast and just, about that car business, the bump to his Volvo.

Larry and Ramona and I sit in the back, and read. We turn north at Tallulah and head up into the Delta. Lucian claps his hands at turtles sunning on logs, and shouts boo at them. A few spill clumsily into the water, but most remain, and watch back. Even the turtles can sense that he is an easier touch.

I nod off, listening to Jim and Lucian discuss recipes. They are talking about food. I awaken at dusk. They're still talking: discussing the weather, which is clear, and hot. They are worrying about nothing more than the shelter over their heads. We are all slowing down, not just Lucian, and it feels good, this day, and is what spring is for.

Gas is seventy-one cents a gallon. Most of the highway is in shadow. Fat times. Our van moves down the road, pulling a trailer of canoes behind it. Plowed fields. Tractor stores. Somewhere, a skunk has been surprised. Patches of late-day sun wash across our faces, our arms, occasionally. The skunk scent wanes and thins to nothing. Jim lights a cigarette. Then after a while there is the smell of a barbecue cookout. Then it goes away, and we're driving on, farther on, and then into the night, and all the windows are down. We trade drivers, and chide each other's abilities and inaccuracies. Lucian cannot find second gear, and we razz him. The teeth of gears grind in pain. Neutral, third, reverse: start over, look again. It is fun to razz him. We dread secretly when it will be our turn to drive, and to search for the wretched, second, hidden gear. We stop once, for ice cream cones. Chocolate. Strawberry.

In Russellville, we meet Adrian. Her hug on Jim is like something from a movie. Time to study the tops of our tennis shoes: examine the tires on the trailer. Things are certified; we have driven six-and-a-half hours, and met her at the precise time we said we would. We drive on.

My turn to thunk and miss, slam and grope. The back of the van is a den of derision. I finally skip it, go from first to third, and we shudder slowly up the dark hills, into the mountains. Lucian allows as to how it is a pain to set up a tent in the dark, but how nice it will be that there's no rain. We don't want to get wet.

Breakfast on top of the hill looking out at the Ozarks: the Mockingbird Cafe. Lucian has found second gear, in his storytelling. A man who slept with his eyes wide open, and had tears all over his bed in the morning, every night, in the army. A Cajun who could chase away mean dogs by dancing, and showing them the palms of his hands. Even the waitress is listening. The coffee is good. There is a hummingbird outside. It is early, and sunny, and the breakfasts are all below three dollars. The river up the road, the one we're going to, is cutting and filling, and flooding and scouring, every year, changing, but we are fat and slow, this morning, this trip, these years. Larry's bacon is as thick as a stack of twenty one-dollar bills. He closes his eyes in bliss as he sits next to Lucian and chews it, because Lucian has decided to stop eating bacon.

Coconut smells of lotion, and the sun so warm. Green trees rising over the river, willows. We've assembled and merged, from all the different places. Ron and Sharon, and Ed and Hannah, from the Coast. The James brothers, from Tennessee. Doc and Bill. Everyone's canoe is green. Everything is a fit. Many people are walking around in movie sunglasses such as the ones Movie Stars sometimes wear, but they are not from our group. There is an abundance too of shorts with flowers on them. But we will leave all that, if we are patient.

Canoes line the shore like a war party: all the noses pointing at the identical angle, downstream. A low-water bridge with magic thick sunlight of green spilling beneath it, onto the water: little gnat bugs swarm and dance, in the light, and also back in the shadows. People wade around in the river. Water slides over wet calves. The sun's so warm. I pick up a stone and press it to my cheek, then to the side of my nose. It feels good, and is hot. I glance up and see Lucian is watching.

One of the boats of flowered-shorts people pushes off, launches, paddles four strokes and turns over. Doc is choking; he is trying to catch his breath, he's laughing so hard. He is making gasping sounds. He is happy. The water is cold. We are all happy. A few kayakers nose around in the green light beneath the bridge, it's as if in France. Ed drives up from the shuttle, which went smoothly, and we are ready. There is a sudden sweetness in my teeth, like candy. I feel dizzy, and salivate and swallow and it passes but when I put the paddle in the water and make the first pull it rises again. In my teeth. A butterfly, blue, moves across the water in front of us. I'm paddling with Larry.

This isn't a hard river. This is an easy river. We have paddled rivers with large waves and angry rocks and fast currents. This is a nice river, with fast steady turns and little rumbling rock-spilled stretches, little spits of cold waves lapping up into the bow, but it is nice, and a sun so hot. We have lunch on a willow island and watch pilgrims float by, separated from their canoes. One of them has a black dog that scrambles along beside him and his wife, following them and their paddles downstream, leaving wet tracks on the pale rocks and boulders as he trots, watching them and not where he is going. Some of them bicker, but there isn't any need for it, really.

"It was her fault," one of them shouts to us, as he drifts by, pointing ahead to his wife, who is cursing the paddle.

"This is the worst paddle I've ever used," she snarls. Her hair is wet, and she is bobbing up and down like an angry bottle, she's being pulled away from us, she's gone. Our sandwiches are good, and dry.

Although we do not know it, there is a woman on the river who can imitate a buzzard, and she is in our midst. We are alarmed to hear Hannah when she first begins, a deep hearty woofing, more of a bark, and think that she is having a sort of seizure. But she's just demonstrating, she worked with one at the zoo once, and they bark like dogs when they are angry. Says she. Lucian looks mildly covetous of this fact: it is a story to go with his others.

We all practice: seven boats, fourteen barking people, paddling down the river. We're safe from pirates.

Such a good and firm river, and flow. When you stop and get out, and step into it, minnows dart against your ankles and bounce off.

Campfire. The bluffs above us, on the river, shine white, like, forgive me, the largest drive-in movie screen in the world, with nothing playing, except a dark ring of trees at the top, and then beautiful stars above that. I'm trying to finish cooking, but Hannah keeps taking my stacked wood and is putting it on the large community fire that we will soon light and gather around. She thinks she is finding easy, wild, free wood and can not get over how abundant it is and how quick she is to find it, and I do not have the heart to tell her. Lucian comes back from the darkness with a medium-sized tree over one shoulder, a tree such as you might climb, to escape from a bear: nothing spectacular, just a tree. Earth and gravel crumbles from the splayed root network, and it is a dead tree, and we'll be warm, tonight. We throw twiggie-bits on the fire after it is lit, and talk. Lucian tells an old story that he must be tired of but as we all want to hear it again he goes inside it and makes it fresh one more time, for our sakes, and it seems this time is the best we've ever heard it. There's a stump, an old tree, rotting down on the beach below us, and we find ourselves, all of us, slowly at first, but then a fusillade—sparks of flint against gravel, skitting over the beach like firecrackers when we miss— hurling stones, from our sitting positions, at this alarmed, solitary stump: solid thunks into its trunk. We're on a gravel bar full of perfect rock-throwing-sized stones, and for five minutes we hurl and wing, all of us, a barrage, chips of wood flying, jobs and supervisors and schedules flying off the ends of our fingertips, until one stone goes wildly past and strikes an aluminum canoe beyond, one of ours pulled up on the shore: the noise startles us, and we cease almost immediately, our arms tingling from the exercise, and we look around at each other sheepishly, and giggle, a little.

Rivers make eddies, curl back around upstream often, and do not always try to get, immediately, to where it is they are headed.

In the morning the way the leaves on the trees droop tells us it is going to rain. The pale green leaves of the poison ivy hang as if scolded, and yesterday they were crisp. Wind moves down the river, racing across the top. Lucian shaves, squatting before a tiny mirror with lather on his face, and Ed shaves too, electrically, down by the water. These delicacies. Bacon snaps and pops and smells good. It is Jim's in his skillet and untended, and Larry and I throw little sassafras spur-berries at it, pretending we want to hit it, but terrified when we come too close.

We paddle beneath the most purple sky, and with wind, and thunder. We reach Hemmed-In Hollow, and get out, and hike up the trail to its spray and dizzyingly high waterfall. Crows fly through the woods. A storm is coming. There are wildflowers, and blossoms. A black snake crosses the path, going down the hill. The trees' tops are bending, in the wind. It's on our faces. When we get there we look at the small waterfall that sails out over the cliff so far above us, our necks craned straight up to see it, our backs and knees bent too, and then we return. Lunch on a bar. The water's dark and deep, on either side of us, and fast. Paddling on, then. We reach our field, our pasture, and set up tents, a dining fly. The storm hits. We sit under the fly's dryness and laugh at it, and shout to be heard over the storm's loudness. We ridicule Larry's green tent, razz it with three z's. It is state-of-the-art, technologically slim, expensive, fashionable, and leaks. It's just a one-man tube, into which the sleeping bag slides; there's a mouth-sized swatch of netting, through which to breathe. It's not a thing you'd even want to be buried in. Like a glove over a finger, it envelops his sleeping bag: that's all. It's green, like a luna moth. It lies there, in the shape of a body, taking the storm's fury, getting wetter and muddier as the fierce raindrops attack it, pummel it. We eat peanuts, bananas, crackers. The rain stops. Larry goes out and turns his tent/bag over: rolls it, with his toe, like a log.

We cook supper: build a fire. Talk: tell jokes. Hardy has forgotten all his good jokes, every one he's ever heard, and strains, reaches deep, but comes up mute. Others remember, however, and carry the slack. Those of us who never knew any in the first place, listen, luxuriously. We start to yawn, too, later. When everyone is in their tents, it rains again, and blows hard that night, obligingly putting the fire out.

Cold in the morning, a forty-degree temperature drop, and we get to wear the heavy clothes we'd been packing along. Jim and Lucian and Ramona and Adrian have been snowed on up here before. By noon, it's eighty again, and we are at the place on the rover where we have to take the canoes out and put them on our trucks and cars and go home.

Adrian's laugh. Jim's smile. Lucian putting the Vulcan death squeeze on Larry's shoulder, and Larry ducking and twisting away to escape it. Sun, on the drive home. Hannah had some strawberries left over, rich and red, big ones, and we snack on them, reach into the plastic bag, and search for the ones dusted with sugar.